The UnWorkbook

CREATIVE READING

Grade 1

by
Becky Daniel-White

Frank Schaffer Publications®

Author: Becky Daniel-White
Editor: Lindsey Lautenbach
Interior Designer: Lori Kibbey

Frank Schaffer Publications®

Send all inquiries to:
Frank Schaffer Publications
3195 Wilson Drive NW
Grand Rapids, Michigan 49544

The UnWorkbook: Creative Reading—grade 1

ISBN: 0-7682-3121-3

1 2 3 4 5 6 7 8 9 10 PAT 10 09 08 07 06 05

Table of Contents

Phonics
7–30

Vocabulary
31–37

Listening Activities
38–53

Main Idea
54–57

Recognizing Words/
Recalling Text
58–67

Inferring/Predicting
68–73

Summarizing/Sequencing
74–77

Compare/Contrast
78–79

Cause/Effect
80–81

Fact/Opinion
82–83

Author's Purpose
84–86

Dramatizing Text
87–90

The Five Ws
and H
91–92

Rhyming
93

 Verbal–Linguistic Intelligence

 Logical–Mathematical Intelligence

 Bodily–Kinesthetic Intelligence

 Visual–Spatial Intelligence

 Musical Intelligence

 Interpersonal Intelligence

 Naturalist Intelligence

0-7682-3121-3 *Creative Reading*

Correlation Chart

	Verbal–Linguistic Intelligence	Logical–Mathematical Intelligence	Bodily–Kinesthetic Intelligence	Visual–Spatial Intelligence	Musical Intelligence	Interpersonal Intelligence	Naturalist Intelligence
Initial Consonants:	7	7	7	7, 9, 11, 12	7, 8, 24	7, 9	
Letter "X":	13	13			13		
Short "A":	14, 15, 16, 18, 26	14, 24	14, 25	14, 15, 16, 25, 26	14, 24, 25	14, 25	
Short "E":	17, 18, 26	24	17, 25	17, 25, 26	17, 24, 25	17, 25	
Short "I":	20, 26, 27	19, 24	25	19, 20, 25, 26	19, 24, 25	19, 24, 25	
Short "O":	22, 26, 27	24	25	22, 25, 26	21, 24, 25	21, 24, 25	21
Short "U":	26, 27	23, 24	23, 25	25, 26	23, 24, 25	23, 24, 25	
Long Vowels:		28–30		28–30	28–30		
Sight Words:	31–38	31, 32, 36		32, 37, 38		31	
Listening for Details:		40, 42, 43	39	39, 41, 42	39–43		39
Listening for Rhymes:		44–46			44–46		
Listening for Sequence:	50	47–49		50	47, 49		47
Listening to Retell:	53			51	51, 52	51–53	52
Reading for Main Idea:	54–57	57		55, 57		54	
Recognizing Action Words:	59, 60		58, 59	59	58	58, 59	
Recognizing Subjects:		61			61		
Recognizing Details:	63	62, 63		62, 63			62
Recalling Text:	64, 65	64	66, 67	65	66, 67		
Making Inferences:	69	68–70	71		69–71	68, 70	
Predicting Outcome:	73	72, 73		73	72	72	
Summarizing:		74		75	74		
Sequencing Events from a Selection:	76, 77	76, 77		76, 77			
Comparing and Contrasting:		78, 79		78, 79		78	
Recognizing Cause and Effect:	81	80, 81		80			
Recognizing Fact and Opinion:	83	82, 83		83	82	82	
Recognizing Author's Purpose:		84, 85		85	84		
Drawing Conclusions:		86		86	86		
Dramatizing Text:	88–90		87–89	90		87	
Who, What, When, Where, Why, and How:	93	91, 93			91, 92	91, 92	

0-7682-3121-3 *Creative Reading*

Introduction

Welcome to the *UnWorkbook*! This unique series endeavors to give you nontraditional ways to teach children a few of the many skills involved in reading. This is not meant to be a sit-at-your-desk worksheet book. Instead, this book offers unique and interactive learning activities and tools to reach children through many different modalities and intelligences.

In these pages you will find lessons to help your students think, look, move, create, and enjoy learning. As people, we all have different times when we understand a concept, that *aha!* moment when we truly grasp the idea. This book offers lessons in reading meant to promote many *aha!* moments in your students.

Traditional Skills, Non-Traditional Instruction

Use this book to teach reading skills to the whole child. The book can broaden the way your students learn and the way you teach them. Let the activities in this book unlock how your students' minds and spirits tick. Get your students out of their seats and encourage them use their whole selves to think and learn. The reading skills covered in this book are traditional, but the methods most definitely are not!

To help you find the specific activities that match your reading skill objectives, use the correlation chart on page four. The activities are listed by skill, by intelligence, and by page number. As many of the activities can be used to teach multiple skills, the activities are cross-referenced in the chart. Some of the basic skills addressed are listed below.

Main Idea and Details	Predicting	Inferencing	Summarizing	Sequencing
What's going on here?	Can you tell what will happen?	Clues offer conclusions!	What happened? Sum it up!	In what order did things happen?

The Multiple Intelligences

Verbal-Linguistic Intelligence

Logical-Mathematical Intelligence

Bodily-Kinesthetic Intelligence

Visual-Spatial Intelligence

Musical Intelligence

Interpersonal Intelligence

Naturalist Intelligence

Introduction

Compare and Contrast	Cause and Effect	Fact and Opinion	Author's Purpose	Story Elements
Compare things that are the same. Contrast their differences.	Why something happened. What happened next?	Can you prove it? Or is it something that's felt or thought?	What does the author mean?	Start simple: people, plot, place, time, point of view.

Adapting for Individual Learning Styles

Many of the lessons in this book are naturally differentiated for differing levels of ability. Some of the words, sentences, or examples, however, are more difficult than others. These are offered to you, the teacher, to use with children of higher abilities at your discretion.

Always change or add to the lessons as you choose. As the teacher, you know that all other things being equal, it is the teacher that makes the difference. Thank you for making a difference to children. Please use this book as a tool in your bag of teaching tricks to reach each child, to meet him where he is, and bring him into the light of *aha's*.

In the crunch for time and preparation for standardized tests, please mix these memorable lessons with more formal work in reading. Learning should be fun and exciting. We hope these lessons will add to learning fun, excitement, and many, many *aha's*.

0-7682-3121-3 *Creative Reading*

Sound of the Day

Each day for four school weeks, center activities around one particular consonant sound (with the exception of letter "X"). Involve parents in their child's learning by sending home the Parent Letter (page 10) and the song "Noisy Letters" (page 8).

Sing the Sound of the Day

Begin each lesson by singing the appropriate verse of "Noisy Letters" (page 8) and reviewing verses for consonant sounds already introduced.

Sharing the Sound of the Day

Encourage students to bring an object that begins with the sound of the day. Students will stand and share their object. Each day, make a list of the objects students have brought in.

Classifying the Sounds

Materials: pencils, 11" by 17" drawing paper, markers or crayons

Directions:

1. Name a category. Students are to name appropriate objects that begin with the sound of the day.

   Examples for "B" include:
   - animals—bees, bears, beetles, bulls, blackbirds
   - fruits—bananas, berries
   - animal sounds—bray, buzz, boom, bark, bleat, baa

2. Pair students. Each pair draws and colors examples of objects that begin with the sound of the day and fit into a particular category. Sample categories: animals, food, colors, clothes, sounds, flowers, plants, toys.

3. In a large group, student pairs share their picture. The class then guesses the categories.

Treasure Boxes

Materials: small boxes, foil gift wrap, scissors, glue sticks, glitter, stickers

Directions: In lessons that follow, students will be given small word cards. In order to keep all of their cards together, each student needs a 3" by 5" box.

1. Students are to decorate their boxes to look like treasure chests.
2. Remind students that the words they can read are their treasures.

0-7682-3121-3 *Creative Reading*

♫ Noisy Letters

Preparation: Teach students the song "Noisy Letters."

Noisy Letters
(Sing to the tune: "Frère Jacques")

Letters are noisy.

Letters are noisy.

They make sounds.

They make sounds.

Letter "B" is buzzing.

Letter "B" is buzzing.

Buzz, buzz, "B."

Buzz, buzz, "B."

Verses:

Letter "C" is cackling	cackle, cackle, "C"
Letter "D" is dinging	ding, ding, "D"
Letter "F" is fizzing	fizz, fizz, "F"
Letter "G" is giggling	giggle, giggle, "G"
Letter "H" is hissing	hiss, hiss, "H"
Letter "J" is jingling	jingle, jingle, "J"
Letter "K" is kissing	kiss, kiss, "K"
Letter "L" is lapping	lap, lap, "L"
Letter "M" is mooing	moo, moo, "M"
Letter "N" is neighing	neigh, neigh, "N"
Letter "P" is purring	purr, purr, "P"
Letter "Qu" is quacking	quack, quack, "Qu"
Letter "R" is ringing	ring, ring, "R"
Letter "S" is sizzling	sizzle, sizzle, "S"
Letter "T" is tooting	toot, toot, "T"
Letter "V" is vrooming	vroom, vroom, "V"
Letter "W" is woofing	woof, woof, "W"
Letter "Y" is yapping	yap, yap, "Y"
Letter "Z" is zooming	zoom, zoom, "Z"

For More Fun!

After students learn all the verses, hold up a letter card. Students sing only the sound line—buzz, buzz, "B;" zoom, zoom "Z."

Published by Frank Schaffer Publications. Copyright protected.

0-7682-3121-3 *Creative Reading*

Sounds of the Day Display

Materials: wall or large bulletin board (the bigger the better), bulletin board paper, pencil, paints, markers

Directions:

1. Cover the area with bulletin board paper.
2. Divide area into seven columns and three rows—21 spaces.
3. Use a marker to write an initial consonant in each space.
4. Students draw and color appropriate pictures in each space.

Examples:

"B"—a boxcar of baskets (berries, bees, bonnets, beans)
"C"—a case of carrots (cars, cards, cantaloupe, cakes)
"D"—a dozen ducks (deer, dragonflies, dogs, drums) in a row
"F"—five fat, flapping flamingos (fish, fleas, flies, frogs)
"J"—a jar of jelly (jacks, jam, jellyfish)
"K"—kitchen full of kiwis (kangaroos, katydids, kayaks, kings)
"L"—a living room full of leopards (lions, llamas, lobsters, loons)
"M"—a mountain of marshmallows (mangoes, magpies, moles)
"P"—a pie full of peaches (pudding, pears, plums, peas, pandas)
"Qu"—a quilt with quail (queens, quince) designs
"T"—a trunk full of tigers (TVs, teeth, tomatoes, turtles)
"W"—a wagon of watermelons (walrus, wallabies, wasps)
"Y"—a yellow yak playing with a yo-yo
"Z"—a zoo full of zebras

Consonant Zoo Rummy

Materials: *Consonant Zoo Cards* (pages 11–12)

Preparation: Copy pages 11 and 12 on heavy cardstock for each student. Students are to color their cards and initial the back of each one.

Rules:

1. Play like rummy.
2. Four children shuffle all of their *Consonant Zoo Cards* (80 cards—four of each letter).
3. Dealer deals seven cards to each player.
4. Players take turns drawing and discarding to make a set of four or a set of three matching consonants. The first to do so is declared the winner.

0-7682-3121-3 *Creative Reading*

Dear Family,

For the next month, our first-grade class will be celebrating the sounds of initial consonants. Here are some fun ideas to help you introduce and reinforce the sounds of the consonants with your child.

- Provide your child with a small box for holding word cards.
- Assist her/him each day in finding something to share that begins with the appropriate sound.
- Encourage your child to choose clothes that might reflect the sound of the day. Example: On "R" day, she might wear red or rubber boots.
- Ask your child about the class activities for the sound of the day.
- Point out objects in the home that begin with the sound of the day.
- Take outings to see or buy things beginning with the appropriate sound.
- The zoo is especially good for reinforcing initial consonant sounds. Name animals and animal sounds that begin with various sounds.
- Provide the class with a special treat that begins with the sound of the day. If you plan to send a class snack, please let us know which day we can expect the special treat, and I will reserve that day for you.
- Each day, ask your child to sing that day's verse of "Letters Make Sounds."

For your convenience, the Sound of the Day schedule follows:

First Week:

Monday—"B" as in ball

Tuesday—"C" as in cat

Wednesday—"D" as in dog

Thursday—"F" as in fun

Friday—"G" as in gate

Third Week:

Monday—"N" as in nut

Tuesday—"P" as in pat

Wednesday—"Qu" as in quiet

Thursday—"R" as in run

Friday—"S" as in sun

Second Week:

Monday—"H" as in hat

Tuesday—"J" as in jog

Wednesday—"K" as in kitten

Thursday—"L" as in lamb

Friday—"M" as in me

Fourth Week:

Monday—"T" as in tan

Tuesday—"V" as in van

Wednesday—"W" as in wax

Thursday—"Y" as in yes

Friday—"Z" as in zoo

Thank you,

b  butterfly

c  cow

d  duck

f  frog

g  goat

h  hen

j  jaguar

k  kangaroo

l  lamb

m mice

Published by Frank Schaffer Publications. Copyright protected.

0-7682-3121-3 *Creative Reading*

Initial Consonants

n
newt

p
pig

q
quail

r
rat

s
seal

t
toucan

v
vulture

W
whale

y
yak

z
zebra

0-7682-3121-3 *Creative Reading*

The Mysterious Letter

Preparation: Wear sunglasses, a cape, or trench coat—some way to make yourself look mysterious. With great fanfare, and in a mysterious voice, say, "I am a mystery letter. You must guess my name." One at a time, give the clues and dramatically write the letters mentioned on the board.

Hints:

1. I rarely say my own name. You can't make me tell you. No, never, never, never! What letter am I?

2. If a word begins with me, I disguise myself by sounding like a completely different letter—the letter "z." What letter am I?

3. If I end a word, I disguise myself by sounding like two completely different letters— "ks." Can you guess my name?

4. The only way you can get me to say my name is to put the letter "e" in front of me, or put a hyphen between me and the rest of a word. Can you guess my name now?

Xylophone—An Excellent Instrument

Preparation: Index cards should be marked: "X," "Z," or "KS." Pass out cards.

Directions:

1. Play a xylophone or show a picture of one. Ask, "Who knows the name of this instrument? Who knows the initial consonant (starting letter) of the word *xylophone*?"

2. Explain that the letter "X" sounds like its name if it has a space or hyphen between it and the rest of the word. Example: *X-ray*

3. Write the letters "KS" on the board. Ask a student to read the sound. Explain that when a word ends in "X" it sounds like "ks." Examples: *box* and *fox*

4. Explain that when a word begins with the "x" sound, it has an "E" before the "X". "Ex" sounds like "X." Examples: *extra, exit, exterminator, excite*

5. Say words containing an "X." Students hold up the appropriate card to show the sound of the "X."

   Examples: *box, x-ray, xylophone, fox, Xerox* (z and ks)

Clap on Short "A"

Directions:

1. Explain that the short "A" sound is the first sound in the word *at*.
2. Have students make the short "A" sound by starting to say "at," but leaving off the sound of the letter "T."
3. Name three-letter words.
4. If the word contains a short "A" sound in the middle, students clap. If the vowel sound isn't the short "A," students remain silent.

   Examples: *sat, sun, bat, big, gun, bet, cat, fun, fan, men, man, can, cap*
5. Next, slowly say the nursery rhyme, "Pat-a-Cake, Pat-a-Cake." Students are to clap each time they hear a short "A."

   Pat-a-cake, pat-a-cake, baker's man!
   Make me a cake as fast as you can.
   Pat it, and prick it, and mark it with a B,
   And there will be enough for Baby and me.

Short "A" Relay

Materials: paper (one large sheet per student), wide-tipped black marker

Preparation: Write the short vowel "A" on six sheets of paper. Make the letters nearly as big as the paper. On the other sheets, write one of the consonants: *b, c, h, j, m, n, r, s,* or *t*. Make enough so that every student can have a consonant or short "A" card.

Directions:

1. Divide into six groups. Give one member of each group a short "A" and each of the others a consonant card.
2. Students are to arrange themselves to spell as many three-letter words as they can and make a list of the words.
3. Meet in a large group and have each group stand holding cards to demonstrate the words they can spell.

Short "A" Word Meter

Materials: *Short "A" Bat Meter*, pencils, paper

Preparation: To increase children's short "A" sight vocabulary, have them make the word meter found on pages 15 and 16.

Directions:

1. Help students make word meters, and show them how to use the meters.
2. As students name words they can make on their word meters, write a master list on the board. Leave up the list.

0-7682-3121-3 *Creative Reading*

Short "A" Bat Meter

Directions:

1. Cut out letter strips (page 16).

2. Cut out short "A" bat.

3. Carefully cut the four slots on the bat. A good way to do this is fold the paper so that you can cut from the middle of the line to the end.

4. Slide cards through slots.

5. Slide both cards to see how many short "A" words you can make.

Short "A" Bat Meter (cont.)

b
d
f
g
h
j
l
m
n
p
r
s
t
v

b
d
g
m
n
p
r
s
t
x

0-7682-3121-3 *Creative Reading*

Ed Is Short "E"

Directions:

1. Explain that the short "E" sound is the first sound in the name *Ed*.

2. Break students into pairs. Pairs take turns saying parts of the word: Ed. First one says short "E" and the other says the sound of letter "D."

3. In a like manner, have students cooperate to say the individual sounds in short "E" words: *r-e-d, h-e-n, p-e-t, b-e-d, b-e-t, m-e-t, w-e-b, T-e-d*.

Little Red Hen

Directions:

1. Read the story to the students. Each time they hear a short "E," they are to cluck softly three times, like a hen.

2. Reread the story to the students. This time, when you get to a short "E" word, pause and let them fill in the word(s).

3. On the board, list the short "E" words in the story. Read the list aloud.

Once upon a time there was a little red hen who wanted some bread. So she went to get her friends, Miss Wren and Mr. Spider. She hoped they could help.

"Not I," said Miss Wren. "I have eggs upon which I must sit."

"Not I, my pet," said Spider. "I have a web to weave."

So the little red hen left her friends and went home to bake by herself. When the bread was baked her friends knocked. "Let us in. We are hungry."

"No," said Little Red Hen. "Go sit on your eggs and spin your web. You do not get a crumb of my bread."

Short "A" and "E" Fun

Materials: lunch sack, *Short "A" and "E" Word Cards*

Preparation: Reproduce and cut apart the word cards on page 18. Fold each and place in a paper lunch sack.

Directions:

1. Players take turns drawing a word.

2. To be sure a student can read the card, she is to whisper it to you.

3. Students may use any method of communicating: pantomiming, saying any words except the word on the card, or drawing a picture on the board.

4. The person who correctly guesses the word gets to be "It" next.

0-7682-3121-3 *Creative Reading*

Short "A" and "E" Word Cards

bed	beg	bet	dad
den	bat	fed	get
hat	hem	hen	man
leg	bag	let	men
cat	mat	nap	net
pat	pen	pet	red
sat	ten	van	vet
web	wed	wet	yes
set	fan	yet	zap
cap	pep	gas	jam
jar	ran	rap	sad

0-7682-3121-3 *Creative Reading*

It Is Short "I"

Directions:

1. Explain that short "I" is the first sound heard in *it*.
2. Students are to take turns naming words that begin with short "I."
3. List them on the board. **Examples:** *if, ill, in, inch, Indian, itch, icky, is, it, its, itself*

Roll 'Em

Materials: *Short "I" Word Cubes*, scissors, glue

Prepare: Reproduce page 20 for each student.

Directions:

1. Students are to cut on solid lines and fold on dotted lines.
2. Spread glue on areas with instructions. The bottom square without a letter will be glued to backside of the top letter.
3. The strip with the other two glued areas must be tucked inside the cube so the glue is attached to the backside of the letters.
4. Use letter cubes to play a short "I" word game. Demonstrate to students that the lowercase "d" can be used as a "p."
5. Follow up games by having students list on the board all the words they made. Short "I" words that can be made with the cubes include: *bid, big, bit, bin, did, dig, dim, dip, hid, him, hip, his, hit, lid, lip, lit, mid, nip, pig, pin, pit, rid, rig, rim, rip, sin, sip, sit, tip*

Game Rules:

1. Each player needs his letter cubes and a pencil and paper.
2. Players take turns rolling cubes and using the two letters facing up to make short "I" words.
3. Example: If a player rolls a "B" and a "G," she can make the word big.
4. Each time a player makes a word, she writes it on her list. It is possible for a player to make two words. Example: If he rolls a "D" and an "M," he can spell *mid* and *dim*.
5. Continue taking turns rolling the cube and making words until one player has ten points or time is called. If time is called, the player with the most short "I" words on her list is declared the winner.

For More Fun!

Use the cubes to practice short "A" and short "E" words, too. Play the game in the same way.

Name _____ **Date** _____

Short "I" Word Cubes

h	b	"p" will overlap here	s	paste to back of "h"

h				
l				
p				
r				
tuck in and paste behind "h"				

g	d	"n" will overlap here	s	paste to back of "g"

g				
m				
n				
t				
tuck in and paste behind "g"				

0-7682-3121-3 _Creative Reading_

Short "O" Is Odd

Directions:

1. Explain that a short "O" is the first sound heard in *odd*.

2. As you list them on the board, students are to take turns naming three-letter words that have a short "O" in the middle.

3. Write "cot" on the board. Ask, "Can you name other words that rhyme with cot?" (hot, dot, got, jot, lot, and so on)

4. On the board list the words: *bob, cop, sod,* and *tot*.

5. Students are to make a list of rhyming words for each word.

6. Allow time for students to make lists.

7. Meet in small cooperative groups to combine lists into a master list. Which group can come up with the most rhyming short "O" words?

   Answers:

   bob: *cob, job, mob, rob, sob*

   cop: *hop, mop, pop, sop, top*

   sod: *cod, God, nod, odd, pod, rod*

   tot: *cot, dot, got, hot, lot, not, pot, rot*

Body Language

Directions:

1. Go outside.

2. Break into groups of threes.

3. Each group is to think of a three-letter short "O" word.

4. Next they are to lie down on the ground and try to form the word with their bodies. Example for *pop*: student in the middle rolls into a ball. The other two use arms to make a loop and their bodies to make the line of the letter "p."

5. Allow time for each group to demonstrate its word to the others, who are to guess what the word is.

Name _____   **Date** _____

Illustrating Short "O" Words

Directions: Read the words in each box. Draw appropriate pictures.

The ox said, "It's not hot!"	Dot put a mop and a top in a box.
Bob got lobster and corn on the cob.	A fox sat in a box and drank pop.

0-7682-3121-3 _Creative Reading_

Umbrella Up

Materials: umbrella

Directions:

1. Put up an umbrella and say, "Umbrella up."

2. Explain that the short "U" sound is the first sound in *umbrella* and *up*.

3. Play a listening game. As you say a three-letter word, students stand up if they hear a short "U" in the middle. If the vowel sound in the word is a not short "U," they are to remain seated.

4. Review other short vowel sounds, too. Say, "No one is standing. Right! That word didn't have a short "U" sound." Ask, "What is the short sound in that word?"

    Examples: *but, cub, cup, cut, dug, fun, gum, hub, hug, hum, hut, jug, mud, nut, pup, rub, rug, run, rut, sum, sun, tub, tug*

Clues That Count

Directions:

1. Break into four teams.

2. One at a time, give clues to short "U" words. The first team member to raise a hand gets to guess.

3. A correct answer wins three points. An incorrect answer means that the team loses a point.

4. Keep score on the board.

Short "U" Puzzles

- shines during the day (sun)
- something to chew (gum)
- a baby dog (pup)
- squishes between your toes (mud)
- a kind of boat (tug)
- a place to take a bath (tub)
- a container for lemonade (jug)
- a shelter made of straw (hut)
- something to crack open (nut)

- a hole in the road (rut)
- a little insect (bug)
- hamburger ingredient (bun)
- one way to get to school (bus)
- opposite of down (up)
- a long sandwich (sub)
- a baby bear (cub)
- another word for slice (cut)
- center of a wheel (hub)

0-7682-3121-3 *Creative Reading*

Short Vowel Sounds

Preparation: Teach students the song, "Short Vowel Sounds."

Short Vowel Sounds

(Sing to the tune: "The Wheels on the Bus")

The vowel in *cat*, is the short "A" sound.

Short "A" sound. Short "A" sound.

The vowel in *cat*, is the short "A" sound.

(*Sing short "A" sound five times.*)

The vowel in *hen*, is the short "E" sound.

Short "E" sound. Short "E" sound.

The vowel in *hen*, is the short "E" sound.

(*Sing short "E" sound five times.*)

The vowel in *pig*, is the short "I" sound.

Short "I" sound. Short "I" sound.

The vowel in *pig*, is the short "I" sound.

(*Sing short "I" sound five times.*)

The vowel in *fox*, is the short "O" sound.

Short "O" sound. Short "O" sound.

The vowel in *fox*, is the short "O" sound.

(*Sing short "O" sound five times.*)

The vowel in *pup*, is the short "U" sound.

Short "U" sound. Short "U" sound.

The vowel in *pup*, is the short "U" sound.

(*Sing short "U" sound five times.*)

Directions:

1. Use the song to play a guessing game.

2. Sing a variety of short vowel animals: *duck, hen, rat, cat, bat, yak, fish, lobster, mink, dog, lamb, wren, cub*

3. Students respond by singing the appropriate vowel sound.

Short "I," "O," and "U" Word Cards

Materials: *Short "I," "O," and "U" Word Cards*

Preparation: Reproduce page 27 for each student. Cut apart cards.

Directions:

1. Students are to initial the back of each of their cards.

2. Have students work in pairs, reading the words to each other.

3. Each student is to place these short vowel word cards in his box with the short "A" and "E" word cards.

0-7682-3121-3 *Creative Reading*

Word Makers

Materials: *Short "I" Words Cubes*, scissors, glue, pencils, paper

Prepare: Reproduce page 20 for each student.

Directions:

1. Players take turns rolling cubes and using the two letters to make as many short vowel words as they can. Example: If a player rolls a "t" and a "p," she can make: *tap, tip, ton, pat, pet, pit, put, dot* (turn the "p" upside down to make the lowercase "d").

2. Each time a player makes a word, she adds it to her list.

3. Continue playing until one player has twenty-five words or time is called.

4. If time is called, the player with the most short vowel words on her list is declared the winner.

Listening for Short Vowels

cat   hen   pig   fox   pup

Preparation: Draw five animals on the board: cat, hen, pig, fox, pup. Write each animal's short vowel name.

Directions:

1. Name short vowel words.

2. Students are to use animal sounds and signals to tell which short vowel sound they hear.

3. Indicate short vowels like this:

> "A" —meowing like a cat
> "E"—flap "wings" and cluck like a hen
> "I"—oink and snort like a pig
> "O"—crawl and sniff like a fox
> "U"—pant and yelp like a puppy

Examples:

Short "A": *bat, cab, can, jam, man, mat, nab, sat*

Short "E": *bed, beg, bet, den, egg, fed, get, hem, jet, leg, less*

Short "I": *bid, big, bit, did, dig, dim, dip, hid, him, hip, his, hit, lid, lip, lit*

Short "O": *cob, job, mob, rob, sob, cop*

Short "U": *but, cub, cup, cut, dug, fun, gum, hub, hug, hum, hut, jug, mud*

0-7682-3121-3 *Creative Reading*

Name _____

Date _____

Cut and Paste Short Vowel Animals

Directions: Cut and paste the animals, according to their short vowels, in the appropriate cage.

a	e
	i
u	o

Published by Frank Schaffer Publications. Copyright protected.

0-7682-3121-3 *Creative Reading*

Short "I," "O," and "U" Word Cards

bid	bug	bit	did
dog	bid	sod	got
hit	hum	hot	bit
log	big	lot	lug
cut	mop	nip	nut
pit	pin	pop	rod
sit	tin	cot	pot
rob	cud	cup	log
sup	fun	pup	zip
hug	hum	hut	jug

0-7682-3121-3 *Creative Reading*

Long Vowels

Directions:

1. Explain that some vowels say their own name.
2. Give examples of long "A" words: *gave, make*.
3. Ask students to name long "A" animals. (ape, snake, snail, whale)
4. Ask students to name long "E" animals. (zebra, beaver, sheep, beetles, bees, geese, peacocks, eagle, beagle)
5. Ask students to name long "I" animals. (lion, tiger, rhinoceros, flies)
6. Ask students to name long "O" animals. (crow, goat, boa, cobra, gopher, mole)
7. Ask students to name a long "U" animal. (mule)

Zoo Bulletin Board

Materials: wall or large bulletin board, bulletin board paper, pencil, paints, markers, construction paper, scissors

Directions: Use a classroom bulletin board to celebrate animals with long vowel sounds.

1. Cover the wall with bulletin board paper.
2. Pass out construction paper.
3. Students are to draw an animal that has a long vowel sound.
4. Color and cut out the animals; attach them to the board.
5. Discuss the names of the animals and their vowel sounds. Ask, "How many of the animals on our board have long "A" sound?" Long "E"? and so on.

0-7682-3121-3 *Creative Reading*

Naming Long Vowels

Preparation: Make eleven columns on the board with headings: Short "A," Short "E," Short "I," Short "O," Short "U," Long"A," Long "E," Long "I," Long "O," Long "U," and "Special Rules."

Directions:

1. One at a time, students are to say their first name. Students are to listen for the first vowel sound in the name.

2. With student input, write each student's first name in the appropriate column. Circle the vowel and put the long or short phonetic mark over it.

3. If the name has a vowel sound changed by a blend, explain that some words have special rules for the sounds of their vowels. Put those names under "Special Rules" column.

   Examples:

   Short "A"—Cameron, Anna, Jasmine   Long "A"—Amaris, Taylor, Grace
   Short "E"—Ella, Ted, Jessa   Long "E"—Leah, Rebecca
   Short "I"—Lily, Tim, Lin   Long "I"— Riley, Rian
   Short "O"—Tom, Rod   Long "O"—Zoe, Olivia
   Short "U"—Dustin, Hunter   Long "U"—Hubert
   "Special Rules"—J[or]dan, [Er]in

Row, Row, Long Vowel Boat

Materials: *Long Vowel Boat*, magazines, scissors, glue sticks

Preparation: Reproduce page 30 five times for each student. Teach students the song below.

Row, Row, Long Vowel Boat
(Sing to the tune: "Row, Row, Row Your Boat")

Row, row, long "A" boat,   Row, row, long "O" boat,
Gently down the stream.   Gently down the stream.
Apes, snakes, snails, and whales,   Gophers, cobras, goats, and crows,
All fit in long "A" boat.   All fit in long "O" boat.

(Repeat song with other vowels.)

Directions:

1. Use the boat patterns to make long vowel books.
2. Students are to draw the animals in the song in the appropriate boats.
3. Students are to give each boat a name with the appropriate sound.
4. Cut and paste other long vowel pictures in the appropriate boat.
5. Make covers for the books and staple along the left-hand edges.

Name

Date

Long Vowel Boat

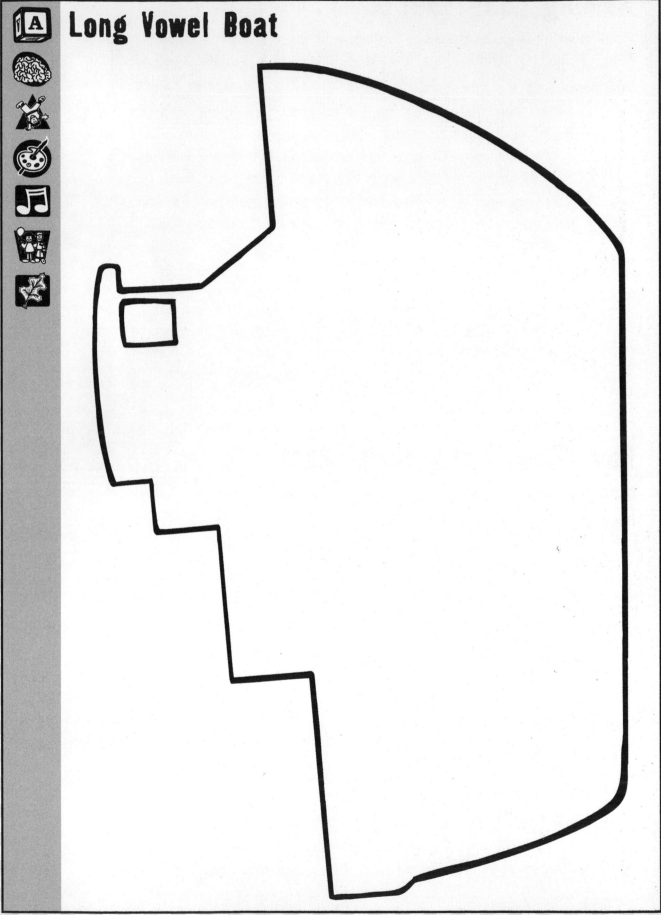

0-7682-3121-3 *Creative Reading*

Sorting It All Out

Materials: *Sight Word Cards*, heavy stock, paper cutter, rubber bands

Preparation: Reproduce pages 33–35 for each student. Cut the word cards apart with a paper cutter and put a rubber band around each set.

Directions:

1. Students are to initial the back of each of their cards.
2. Begin by having students sort the cards according to initial consonants. Then ask, "How many words begin with 'B'? Which initial consonant has the most word cards?"
3. Next, students are to sort the cards with short vowels. How many cards have short "A" sounds? "E"? "I"? "O"? "U"? All together, how many cards have short vowel sounds?
4. Finally, students are to sort out the cards with long vowels. How many cards have long "A" sounds? "E"? "I"? "O"? "U"? All together, how many cards have long vowel sounds?
5. Instruct students to keep their sight word cards in their boxes.

Concentration

Materials: one set of *Sight Word Cards* (per group)

Directions:

1. Divide students into groups of three or four.
2. Mix up the sight word cards and scatter them facedown on the table.
3. Students take turns flipping over a card and reading it.
4. If the player knows the word, she gets to keep it.
5. If she doesn't know the word, the card is placed facedown on the table again.
6. Continue playing until all the cards have been collected by players.
7. The player with the most cards is declared the winner.

Four-Letter Sight Words

Materials: four-letter sight word cards, pencil, paper

Directions:

1. Pair students.
2. Sort the four-letter words from the deck and place them face down.
3. Each player picks up a card and holds onto it.
4. Players take turns asking questions.

   Examples:

   How many vowels?   Does the word have the letter "T"?

   Is the last letter a vowel?   How many consonants?

5. The first player to guess the other's four-letter word wins that round.

0-7682-3121-3 *Creative Reading*

Scrambling Five or More Letters

Materials: *Sight Word Cards* (pages 33–35)

Directions:

1. Explain that you are going to scramble the letters of some of the sight words. (Students may use sight word cards to help them.)
2. Divide students into four teams and choose names for the teams. List team names on the board.
3. One at a time, scramble words on the board. The first person to name a word gets a point for his team.

again—aaing	write—riwte	after—aerft
before—fobeer	down—wodn	could—oucld
every—veery	going—nggoi	funny—unyfn
little—lleitt	please—spelea	there—hrete
think—khint	three—hrete	pretty—ptyret
thank—haknt	under—ruden	would—oduwl

Sight Word Search

Materials: *Sight Word Search*, pencils

Preparation: Reproduce page 36 for each student.

Directions:

1. To reinforce spelling of sight words, use the puzzle as a group activity.
2. Write one of the following sight words on the board.

know	he	in	it	is	new	now	jump	my	not	like
no	of	old	on	look	me	so	saw	away	am	an
but	and	under	big	did	eat	fly	can	find	get	every
down	got	funny	have	said	that	write	some	stop	went	soon
to	two	what	yes	you	your	upon	with	pretty	let	by
the	she	they	run	as	make					

3. Students look for that same arrangement of letters in the puzzle and circle the word. Allow plenty of time for students to find the words.
4. Leave the words up for those who need extra time for searching.
5. On another occasion, let students work the puzzle on their own.

Color Word Rings

Materials: *Color Word Rings*, crayons, scissors, hole punch

Preparation: Reproduce pages 37 and 38 on heavy stock (per student).

Directions: Help students make their Color Word Rings and memorize the color words.

0-7682-3121-3 *Creative Reading*

Sight Word Cards

a	as	again	all
any	ate	away	after
am	be	an	before
but	and	been	both
ask	are	by	at
came	could	big	did
blue	eat	fly	can
find	for	give	from
get	every	down	going
do	funny	have	got

0-7682-3121-3 *Creative Reading*

Sight Word Cards (cont.)

know	her	go	good
him	had	he	his
has	help	here	into
I	in	let	it
is	live	may	new
now	jump	my	not
like	no	of	once
little	old	on	open
then	look	me	please
there	make	one	think
out	saw	take	play

0-7682-3121-3 *Creative Reading*

Sight Word Cards (cont.)

said	read	them	three
tell	the	pretty	she
thank	ran	say	that
round	some	they	want
ride	stop	this	run
so	too	see	went
soon	two	to	under
what	was	when	will
who	well	were	yes
we	write	you	your
up	with	upon	would

0-7682-3121-3 *Creative Reading*

Name _____   **Date** _____

Sight Word Search

Directions: Find and circle as many words as you can. The words are written across, down, or diagonally. How many can you find?

k n o w t a o l f i n d
n e o i h m l i b i g f
o w x t e v d k x g x l
w a s h y e s e v e r y
s o m e s t o p x t o f
a w a y w w o f u n n y
i s u o h r n t w o d c
d y p u a i m s a w i a
p o o n t t a j e g d n
r u n d x e k u a o m e
e r s e l l e m t t b y
t o h r e o i p h a v e
t w e n t o n d o w n x
y t h a t k a n d b u t

0-7682-3121-3 *Creative Reading*

Color Word Rings

Directions:

1. Color the crayons the correct colors.

2. Cut out each crayon.

3. Use a hole punch to put a hole where indicated.

4. Put the color words on a small metal ring.

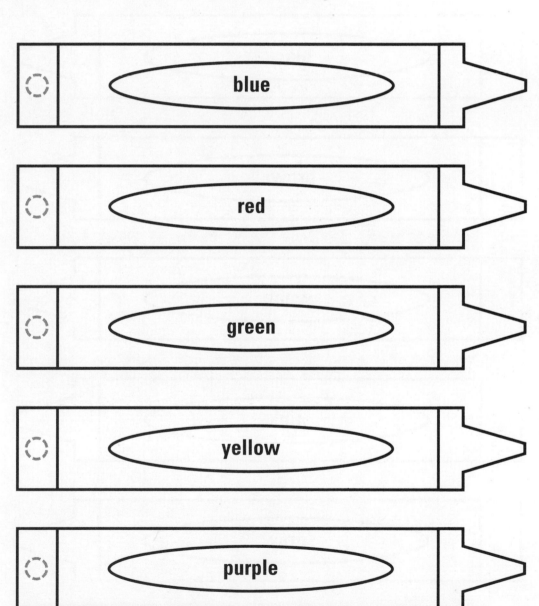

blue

red

green

yellow

purple

Sight Words

0-7682-3121-3 *Creative Reading*

Color Word Rings (cont.)

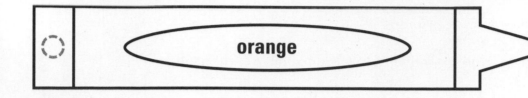

orange

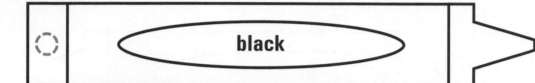

black

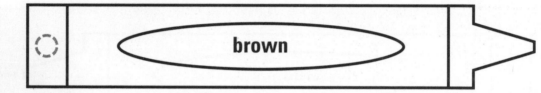

brown

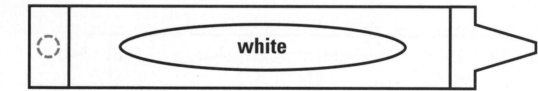

white

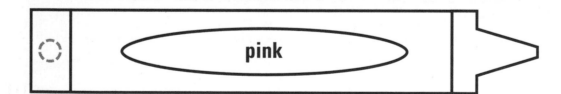

pink

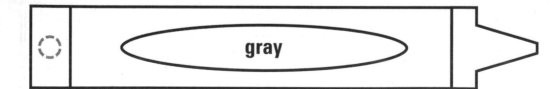

gray

0-7682-3121-3 *Creative Reading*

Teacher Says

Directions: Go outside. As you give directions, students are to follow.

1. Boys stand up and make a single-file line.
2. (Name a boy), move to the front of the line. Lead them around in a circle.
3. All boys go back and sit down.
4. Girls stand and hold hands to make a circle.
5. Drop hands, please.
6. Girls wearing a skirt or dress, step inside the circle.
7. Girls on the outside of the circle, go back and sit down.
8. The rest of the girls go back and sit down, too.
9. All those wearing something red, please stand.
10. Those standing, run in place ten times. Sit down.
11. All those wearing brown shoes, stand and join hands to make a circle.
12. Walk around in the circle until you return to your original place in the circle. Sit down.
13. All those wearing black shoes stand. Run in place twenty times. Sit down.
14. Everyone stand and stretch up. Bend and stretch down. Stand. Sit down and be very still.

Down on the Farm

Materials: *Down on the Farm* reproducible (page 40), crayons in primary and secondary colors

Preparation: Reproduce page 40 for each student. Make sure everyone has red, blue, yellow, green, orange, and purple crayons or markers.

Directions: Give directions and students follow.

1. Use your orange crayon to color the largest animal's body. Use red to color its head.
2. Use your blue crayon to color the middle lamb.
3. Use your purple crayon to color the smallest animal.
4. Use your yellow crayon to color the two mice nearest the snail.
5. Use your green crayon to color the mice in the bottom row.
6. Use your orange crayon to color the first lamb.
7. Use your red crayon to color the only animal with wings.
8. Use your green crayon to color the last lamb.
9. Use your yellow crayon to color the last three mice.

Down on the Farm

0-7682-3121-3 *Creative Reading*

No Clowning Around

Materials: *Clowning Around* worksheet, crayons

Preparation: Reproduce page 42 for each student.

Directions:

1. Pass out clown pictures and make sure each child has crayons or markers in primary and secondary colors.

2. Explain that you will read a story containing details about the picture. You will read the story twice.

3. Students are to use their crayons to color the clowns as you read the story. Explain that they won't have time to color everything as you read. They should just put a color where it belongs so they can complete the picture after the story has been read.

4. Say, "After I read the story two times, you will have time to finish coloring the picture."

5. Slowly read the story to the students. Repeat.

6. Allow ample time for students to finish coloring their pictures.

Clowning Around

Mr. and Mrs. David and their son, Max, are dressed up like clowns. For her costume, Mrs. David cut off and hemmed her husband's old red suit. She made Max a white clown's suit with purple dots.

Mr. David's costume is the most realistic. He rented it. It has a yellow shirt and vest. His pants are orange.

Mrs. David is holding three balloons. Each balloon is one of her favorite colors: purple, orange, or green. She is wearing a yellow wig. Her tie matches her wig.

Mr. David is wearing a green tie and hat. Max's hat matches his suit. The whole family is wearing red shoes and blue socks. Each member of the family has a red nose.

Name _____   **Date** _____

Clowning Around

0-7682-3121-3 *Creative Reading*

Which Is It?

Directions:

1. Explain that you are going to read lists of four words and then ask questions that can be answered with one of the four words.

2. Begin by giving an example: apple, marshmallow, banana, glue. Then ask questions. Always repeat the four words after the question has been answered.
   - Which one is white?
   - Which one is soft?
   - Which one is sticky?

(Encourage creative thinking—even though you expect the answer glue, marshmallows can be sticky, too.)

Examples:

cupcake, watermelon, milk, feather
- Which is usually drunk cold?
- Which is the lightest weight?
- Which has been baked in an oven?
- Which is sometimes sliced into wedges?

paper, flower, sunlight, dill pickle
- Which is warming to your face?
- Which is sometimes sour?
- Which is grown in gardens?
- Which is flat and smooth?

shoe, hat, ice cream cone, blueberry pie
- Which is eaten frozen?
- Which is worn on the head?
- Which is bought in pairs?
- Which is good warm with cream on top?

popcorn, chocolate ice cream, sunglasses, vegetable soup
- Which is light brown and cold?
- Which is good with butter on top?
- Which is a nice winter meal?
- Which is worn on the face?

dog, whale, lion, elephant
- Which is kept as a pet?
- Which has a trunk?
- Which is the fiercest?
- Which lives in water?

0-7682-3121-3 *Creative Reading*

Rhyme Time

Directions:

1. Write a short vowel word on the board. **Example:** bed
2. Ask someone to read it.
3. Explain that rhyming words have the same sound at the end.
4. With input from students, make a list of words that rhyme with bed.
5. One at a time, write other short vowel words on the board.
6. Students name rhyming words as you list them on the board.

Rhymes With

Directions:

1. On the board, draw a simple sketch of the following animals and list their names: pig, cat, snail, fox, fish, snake, hen.
2. Explain that you are going to say some words and students should listen to find out which animal the word rhymes with.
3. When student names the appropriate rhyming animal, let her go to the board and list the word under that animal.

   Examples:

   big, pen, make, take, mail, rail, dig, fog, jail, box, cake, ten, lake, bat, pail, bake, fig, dish, rig, wig, rake, wish, tail, men, nail, den, fail

Mystery Words

Directions:

1. One at a time, give clues to a mystery word including a rhyming word.
2. Students listen to the clues and guess the mystery words.

   Examples:

   a dessert that rhymes with *lie*
   a color that rhymes with *bed*
   a fruit that rhymes with *bandana*
   a vegetable that rhymes with *born*
   a color that rhymes with *sack*
   an ice cream flavor that rhymes with *hint*
   a name that rhymes with *wax*
   fruit that rhymes with *berry*
   an animal that rhymes with *box*
   two animals that rhyme with *cat*

Published by Frank Schaffer Publications. Copyright protected.

0-7682-3121-3 *Creative Reading*

Pick the Two

Directions:

1. Explain that you will be listing groups of four words. Students are to listen for the two words in each group that rhyme.

2. Students take turns naming the two words in each group that rhyme.

3. As rhyming pairs are named, list them on the board.

   Examples:

   cat, boy, toy, back
   mail, to, ten, nail
   ice, fly, six, mix
   candy, cookie, cake, sandy
   paper, pen, ten, crayon
   clip, sip, glue, going
   cow, dog, cat, wow
   finger, arm, farm, leg
   berry, apple, cherry, banana
   blue, red, yellow, mellow
   ink, pink, red, green
   clam, ham, frog, bird
   seven, two, nine, mine
   boy, girl, corn, horn

Nursery Rhymes

Directions:

1. Read or say nursery rhymes.

2. Students are to listen and give the rhyming words.

3. Then ask questions and students must use their memories to think of rhyming words.

   Examples:

   In the nursery rhyme, "Little Miss Muffet," what rhymed with "sat down *beside her*"? (spider)

   In the rhyme, "Little Boy Blue," what rhymed with "*corn*"? (horn)

   In the rhyme, "Pease-Porridge," what rhymed with "pease-porridge *cold*"? (nine days *old*)

   In the rhyme, "Little Jack Horner," what rhymed with "put in his *thumb*"? (pulled out a *plum*)

   In the rhyme, "Heigh, Diddle, Diddle," what rhymed with "heigh, diddle, *diddle*"? (the cat and the *fiddle*)

   In the rhyme, "Jack Be Nimble," what rhymed with "Jack be *quick*"? (*candlestick*)

Sequencing

Materials: paper, pencil

Directions:

1. This game is played with students sitting at their desks with pencils down.

2. You name a sequence of letters, numbers, and words.

3. Student listen and then write the letters, numbers, or words in the order they were given.

4. All pencils down again.

5. Ask two or three questions after each sequence.

   Examples:

   Which letter did I say last?   Which letter came after "A"?

   Which letter was in the middle?   Which letter came before "I"?

6. Write the letters, numbers, and words on the board so students can check their work.

   Examples:

A, V, G	X, Y, Q	B, Z, A
9, 3, 0	3, 7, 5	3, 7, 1
men, hen, ten	cat, bat, rat	red, bed, fed
B, E, R, T	I, V, E, T	B, C, X, A
5, 7, 9, 2	6, 8, 3, 1	12, 16, 68, 6

Echo Me

Directions:

1. To the tune of the first two lines of "Twinkle, Twinkle, Little Star," sing phrases.

2. Students listen and echo them back.

   Examples:

   • Pretty, pretty, Siamese cat—walking on the soft, straw mat.

   • Nervous, worried, little lad—frowning, moping, very sad.

   • Funny donkey, walking tall—would you like to climb the wall?

   • Apple, oranges, peaches, too—all belong in morning stew.

   • Racing rabbits wandered in—berry pie on their fuzzy chins.

   • Master bakers working late—filling pies and baking cakes.

3. Have students sing phrases or lines for others to echo in tunes of their choices.

0-7682-3121-3 *Creative Reading*

Ready, Set, Go!

Directions:

1. Go outside.

2. Give three-part directions. Then say, "Go."

3. Students listen and at the word "Go," they perform the actions.

4. If many have difficulty with a particular sequence, repeat it.

   Examples:
   - Put hands on top of head. Bend at the waist. Touch the ground. Go.
   - Jump up and down three times. Clap twice. Fold arms at waist. Go.
   - March in place ten times. Count to five. Clap once. Go.
   - Flap arms like a bird. Meow like a cat. Jump like a frog. Go.
   - Pretend to play a guitar. Sing the first verse of "Row, Row, Row Your Boat." Pretend to put the guitar back into a case. Go.
   - Scratch your head. Touch knees with hands. Shout "Popeye!" Go.
   - Place hands over ears. Bend head to side. Turn around once. Go.
   - Clap three times. Jump up and down six times. Clap five times. Go.
   - Skip in a circle. Count to ten. Hop on one foot four times. Go.
   - Move arms like swimming. Bark like a dog. Hop like a rabbit. Go.

5. Break into pairs.

6. Students take turns giving each other three-part directions and signaling, "Go."

Zoo Parades

Materials: *Zoo Parade Cards*, paper cutter

Preparation: Reproduce page 48 for each student. Use paper cutter to cut cards apart. Give each student a complete set of nine cards.

Directions:

1. Name a sequence of animals, then say, "Go."

2. In the appropriate sequence, students are to line up the animal cards.

3. When each student has his parade ready, repeat the sequence for each student to check his work.

4. Begin with a sequence of four. Advance to sequences of five, six, or more.

   Examples:
   - An elephant leads the parade. Next comes a rhino, a hippo, and a lamb in that order.
   - An alligator is in front. Next comes a snake, a bird, and an elephant.
   - A zebra is last in line. First in line is a snake. In the middle are a bird and a lion. The bird is in front of the lion.

5. Follow up by having students take turns naming the sequence while others make the parades.

Zoo Parade Cards

0-7682-3121-3 *Creative Reading*

Sarah Baked Brownies

Directions:

1. Slowly read the paragraph aloud twice.
2. Students listen so they can answer sequencing questions.
3. Write one of the questions on the board.
4. List student answers on the board, too.
5. Reread the story to check the answers.
6. Follow up with the worksheet on page 50.

Sarah Baked Brownies

The very first thing Sarah had to do was go to the store to buy the brownie mix and eggs. When she got home, she washed her hands and got out the bowl, spoon, and measuring cup. When she had all the supplies she needed, she opened the brownie mix and poured it into the bowl. She broke two eggs and put them in the mix. She measured a cup of water and added that to the mix. Then she stirred the mixture one hundred times.

Sarah set the oven for 350°. Next she poured the mixture into a baking pan. When the oven was hot, she put the pan into the oven. After 25 minutes, she used oven mitts to pull the brownie pan out of the oven.

Questions:

1. Before Sarah began to bake, what did she have to do?
2. What did she buy at the store?
3. What was the first thing she did when she got home from the store?
4. What was the very last thing Sarah did?
5. What did Sarah put in the bowl first?
6. What did Sarah put in the bowl second?
7. What did Sarah put in the bowl last?
8. What did Sarah do after she stirred the mixture one hundred times?
9. Just before pouring the mixture into a baking pan, what did Sarah do?

Sarah Baked Brownies

Directions: Cut and paste the cards in the correct order. Draw an appropriate picture in each box.

1.	2.
3.	4.
5.	6.

She broke two eggs and put them in the mix.	Sarah went to the store.
Sarah took the brownie pan out of the oven.	Sarah washed her hands.
Sarah stirred the mixture.	She measured one cup of water.

0-7682-3121-3 *Creative Reading*

It's No Joke

Directions:

1. Have students take turns telling their favorite joke.

2. After each student tells his joke, let another student retell the joke.

3. Discuss as a group whether or not the retelling was sequential and contained all the important elements of the original joke.

All in the Family

Directions:

1. One at a time, have six or eight students tell about the people who live in their home. They are to give names and tell a little about each person.

    Example: My mother is a single mother. She is a teacher. I have four brothers, Mark, John, Andrew, and Mike. Mark is in college. John is in high school. Andrew is in junior high. Mike and I go to this school. We walk back and forth to school together.

2. Stories should be approximately fifty words long. If the story begins to ramble, cut it short. Explain that the story might have too many details to be remembered by others.

3. After the story is told, another student retells the story, including names, details, etc.

4. When the story has been retold, ask the storyteller if all the important facts were correct and included.

Illustrating All in the Family

Materials: paper, crayons or markers

Directions:

1. Students are to draw a picture of the people who live in their home.

2. Repeat having six or eight students tell about the people who live in their home. Use the pictures as visual aids for the storytelling.

3. As before, after the story is told, another student retells the story, including names and details.

4. When the story has been retold, ask the original storyteller if all the important facts were correct and included.

5. Discuss whether the stories were easier to remember when a picture was included.

The Secret

Directions:

1. Go outside on the grass.
2. Students are to form a circle by holding hands.
3. Sit down in the grass.
4. Whisper a sentence in one person's ear.
5. That person whispers the secret in the next person's ear.
6. Repeat until the secret comes full circle.
7. Ask the last person to say the secret aloud.
8. Say the original message.
9. Discuss the accuracy of the telling.

   Secrets to Tell:
   - The old gray mare was sold to Farmer Mac for fifteen cents.
   - Some cats like to eat birthday cake and vanilla ice cream.
   - My mother was born in Iowa; my father was born in Texas.
   - On Saturdays I like to sleep in, then drink hot chocolate and read the comics in the paper.
   - Carla said she is moving to Nevada the first week in April.
   - Jack and Jill went down the hill to buy some mosquitoes.
   - Many cooks spoil the broth, but they get the meal done quicker.

10. Follow up by having students make up the secrets to be passed around the circle.

Listening and Retelling Relay

Materials: *Sentence Strips*, paper cutter, paper clips

Preparation: Reproduce the sentence strips on page 53 (one for every five or six students). Stack pages and cut sentence cards apart. Paper clip together the matching sentences.

Directions:

1. Go outside.
2. Break into teams of five or six. (Each team needs to have the same number of players.)
3. Teams line up in a straight line, then sit down in the grass.
4. The first people in line should be your best readers. Give the leader of each group a copy of the same sentence strip.
5. On the count of three, the message is read by the leader and passed along verbally from one team member to the next. When the message reaches the end of the line, teacher listens to the last person to see if he has it letter perfect. If not, the first person begins again.
6. The first team to say the message correctly wins a point.
7. Repeat with the other messages.

0-7682-3121-3 *Creative Reading*

Sentence Strips

A lot of big red ants found the basket of food and attacked it.

My friend Durand will jog to town and back again.

On the way home from work, my mother stops
to shop for meat.

We left the party because we wanted to see
a baseball game on TV.

Andy works so far from home, he has to take a jet to work.

Mary and Abdul have the same color shirt.

Aunt Amy left her blue wig beside her bed and her dog ate it.

The strap on my watch broke just before lunch.

Suzi is having a birthday party, but I will be out of town.

If you ever go to the desert, stop and look at the cactus.

My brother Jamal needs help in math and reading.

0-7682-3121-3 *Creative Reading*

Storytellers

Directions:

1. Choose a person to give the first line of a story. Another person adds a line, the third a third line, and so on.

2. As students give their sentences, record the story on the board.

3. When you come to a good place to stop the story, ask questions that can be answered by words in the story.

4. Students are to come forward and use chalk to underline the words that answer the questions.

   Example:

   Friday my Aunt Reba came to our house. She brought her six large dogs with her. Mother said the dogs had to stay outside. The dogs barked and barked. So that night, Aunt Reba snuck the dogs into her bedroom. When mother found out the dogs slept inside, she was furious. Saturday Aunt Reba and her dogs went home early.

Questions:

- What day of the week did Aunt Reba come for a visit?
- What did Aunt Reba bring with her?
- What did Aunt Reba do when the dogs were shut outside?

Group Stories

Directions:

1. Break into groups of five or six.

2. Choose a person in the first group to give the first line of a story. The second person adds a line, the third a third line, etc.

3. As students give their sentences, write them on a big sheet of paper.

4. Repeat with each group until you have helped all groups write their stories.

5. Students are to ask each other questions that can be answered by reading their story.

6. Students point to the words that answer the questions.

7. In a large group, have a member of each group read their group's story.

0-7682-3121-3 *Creative Reading*

Name _____ **Date** _____

Colorful Animals

Directions: Read and follow the directions.

1. Use your yellow crayon to color the two animals that rhyme with *rat*.

2. Use your blue crayon to color the mule.

3. Use your red crayon to color the two animals that rhyme with *hog*.

4. Use your purple crayon to color the raccoon.

5. Use your green crayon to color the two animals with a short "U" name.

6. Use your blue crayon to color the animal with a short "I" name.

7. Use your orange crayon to color the animal with a short "E" name.

8. Give the zebra pink stripes.

9. Use your purple crayon to color the animal with a long "A" name.

0-7682-3121-3 *Creative Reading*

Pick a Word—Not Any Word

Directions:

1. Write the story "Grandpa's Big Red Barn" on the board.
2. Have students number a paper one to ten.
3. Read the story aloud.
4. Ask questions that can be answered with one (or two) word(s) in the story.
5. Students record the answers on their papers.
6. Follow up by having students draw a picture of Grandpa's farm including as many details as possible.

Grandpa's Big Red Barn

Grandpa has a big, brown mule that pulls the hay wagon. The mule pulls wagon-loads of hay from the field to Grandpa's big, red barn.

Grandpa keeps the hay in the barn loft. Grandpa feeds the hay to his seven cows. Grandma and Grandpa milk the cows every day at sunrise and sunset.

The mule and cows all sleep in the big, red barn with Grandma's orange-striped cat.

Questions:

1. Which of Grandpa's animals is brown?
2. Who helps Grandpa milk the cows?
3. What does the mule pull?
4. How many cows does Grandpa have?
5. Where does Grandpa keep the hay?
6. Which of the animals in the story is orange-striped?
7. How many times a day do the cows get milked?
8. What color is Grandpa's barn?
9. What do the cows eat?
10. All together, how many animals sleep in the barn?

0-7682-3121-3 *Creative Reading*

Read, Think, Color

Directions: Look at the picture and follow the directions.

1. Use a blue crayon to color the thing that is sharp.
2. Use a red crayon to color the fruit.
3. Use a purple crayon to color the thing that needs a string to fly.
4. Use a green crayon to color the things that are alive.
5. Decorate the dessert with pink icing and red candles.
6. Use a white crayon to color the things that are usually white.
7. Use an orange crayon to ring around anything you can eat.

        0-7682-3121-3 *Creative Reading*

Hop, Skip, Jump Away

Directions:

1. Explain that in every sentence, action words tell the movement. Ask for examples of actions and list them on the board.

2. Say, "Girls stand and jump up and down." Then tell them to be seated. Ask, "What did the girls do?" Write "jumped" on the board.

3. Reinforce recognizing action words by having the class follow directions . Each time, discuss the action word and make a list on the board.

   Examples:
   - Blue-eyed kids, stand up and take a bow.
   - Those wearing jeans, clap five times.
   - All boys, stand and stretch. Sit back down.

Can You Do It?

Directions:

1. Explain that if you can do it, it is an action.

2. One at a time, give the words below.

3. If the word is an action, students are to stand up and pantomime the action. If the word is not an action, they are to remain very still.

   Examples:

jump	walk	sing	boy	eight	eat	elephant
key	read	climb	nuts	sunlight	bake	bathe

Movement Guessing Game

Directions:

1. Choose a student. Whisper the name of an animal and the way it moves.

2. Student uses his/her body to move like that animal moves.

3. Class guesses the animals and/or movements.

   Examples:
   - Lope like a llama. (long, easy stride)
   - Trot like a tiger. (jogging gait)
   - Strut like a peacock. (walk proud)
   - Amble like an elephant (leisurely walk, swing arm like a trunk)
   - Sway like a camel. (move back and forth from side to side)
   - Gallop like a gazelle. (both feet off ground at once)
   - Hop like a frog. (jump forward with feet together)
   - Slither like a snake. (on belly, sliding motion)
   - Creep like a turtle. (on all fours move very slowly)

0-7682-3121-3 *Creative Reading*

Action Word Cards

Materials: *Action Word Cards*

Prepare: Reproduce page 60. Cut apart and fold each. Place in a sack.

Directions:

1. Break into four teams.
2. One at a time, a student comes up and draws an action word from the bag.
3. In thirty seconds or less, without speaking, just moving in the appropriate way, she tries to relay the word to her team members.
4. Team members call out action words until they name the correct one. If after time is called, they have not guessed, they do not get a point for that round. Repeat with each team.

Making Sentences

Materials: *Action Word Cards*, paper, pencils

Preparation: Reproduce page 60 for each student. Cut apart and place in treasure boxes with other word cards.

Directions:

1. Break into small, cooperative groups. Working on the floor where there is plenty of room, students use their word cards to make sentences.
2. Each time they make a sentence, a group scribe lists it.
3. Have groups compete to see which group can make the most sentences.
   Examples:
   - The big hen can strut.
   - The little old man will eat.
4. Have each group share their sentences with the other groups.
5. Point out the subject and action word in each sentence.

Sentence Makers

Materials: treasure boxes, word cards

Directions:

1. Now that students know sentences need a subject and action word, give them practice making sentences with their word cards.
2. Challenge students to make the longest sentence they can.
3. Challenge students to make the shortest sentence they can. **Example:** I go.
4. Challenge students to write a sentence with every word beginning with the same consonant. **Example:** Men may march.

0-7682-3121-3 *Creative Reading*

Action Word Cards

walk	gallop	jog	run
skip	stretch	roll	reach
twist	tap	dance	hula
march	strut	flap	stroll
crawl	sneak	hide	wiggle
slide	leap	swim	dress
sway	bathe	dart	loop
creep	sleep	wave	wait
jump	sit	climb	write
eat	kick	scream	eat
draw	toss	bend	hop

0-7682-3121-3 *Creative Reading*

Off the Subject

Materials: pencils, paper

Directions:

1. Explain that the subject of a sentence moves or is moved. Example: I hiked the hill. Ask, "What moved? *I* is the subject of the sentence."

2. List sample sentences on the board.

3. Students are to come up and put a circle around the subject and a box around the action word.

   Sample Sentences:

   David skipped rope.   Ann swam in the pond.
   Becky cleaned the house.   Margo ate her lunch.
   Myra found her pencil.   Tom broke the toy.
   Carla spilled her milk.   Naomi drove the bus.

That's Something

Directions:

1. Remind students that subjects move or are moved.

2. Give more complicated sentences and let students pick out the subjects.

   Examples:

   • The spotted *dog* ran around the yard.
   • *JoAnn and I* went skating after school.
   • *We* ate ice cream and cake at the party.

3. Have students fold their paper horizontally and vertically to make four equal sections. Unfold and number the sections one through four.

4. On the board, write four sentences. Students are to draw a picture of the subjects in each sentence.

Sorting through Treasures

Materials: small boxes, word cards

Directions:

1. Each child is to read through his stack of word cards and sort out the action words. Reserve this stack of cards.

2. Next, each child is now to sort out word cards that are subjects. Have students take turns reading some of the subjects.

3. Using the action cards and subject cards plus other word cards, have students make five complete sentences.

Details, Details, Details

Directions: Explain that details are what makes everyone different. It is the same in a sentence. The details describe the subject or what the subject is doing.

1. Give a sentence: The girl is here. Ask, "What details do we know about the girl?" Then say, "The small, blonde girl is here." Ask, "What details do we know about the girl?" Say, "Details explain and describe things."

2. Go outside and have students point out details such as the color of a building, size of a tree, or shape of a bus.

3. Give a detail and ask the students to point out something that has that detail.

pretty	metal	smooth
rough	noisy	flat
spotted	smelly	shiny
hedged	wet	striped

The Playground

Materials: drawing paper, pencils, markers or crayons

Directions:

1. Go outside. Have students look at the playground and make mental notes of details.

2. Inside the classroom, each student is to draw a picture of the playground including as many details as she can remember.

3. In a large group, discuss the drawings.
   - Did anyone include a detail that everyone else missed?
   - Is there an object nearly everyone included?
   - Did everyone see the same color slide?

Remember the Details

Directions:

1. Ask a member of the class to come forward.

2. The class gets a minute to note details of the person.

3. Then ask the person to leave the room or go where the class cannot see her.

4. Ask and list detail questions on the board along with the variety of answers given by classmates.
   - How is her hair worn?
   - What color are her shoes?
   - Is she wearing socks?
   - Is she wearing a ring?

5. Call the student back to the front of the class. Check answers.

6. Give as many students as possible the opportunity to be "detailed."

0-7682-3121-3 *Creative Reading*

Name   **Date**

Circus Peanuts

Directions: Underline all the words that give details.

How much do you know about Circus Peanuts? Circus Peanuts are orange. They are peanut-shaped. Circus Peanuts are made of marshmallow. They are very sweet.

Circus Peanuts were first made in the 1800s. They were made by many different people. Circus Peanuts used to be sold only in a few places. Now you can buy them all over.

At first, Circus Peanuts were sold only in the spring. In the late 1940s, a good wrapper was made. Today you can buy Circus Peanuts all year long.

What is your favorite candy? Do you like Circus Peanuts best? Draw a dozen Circus Peanuts in a plastic bag.

Now You See It—Now You Don't

Directions:

1. Put a sentence on the board. **Example:** The red dog jumped into the lake and swam to the log.

2. Give students time to read it.

3. Cover the sentence with a strip of paper.

4. Ask questions about the details in the sentence.

What color was the dog?	Where did it jump?
Where did it swim?	How did the dog get to the log?

5. Uncover the sentence and repeat each question.

Sample sentences and questions:

My Aunt Mary is often cross and wears a frown.
- What is the cross woman's name?
- How is the woman related to the speaker?
- What does the woman wear on her face?

Mrs. Lamb let the class take our new reading books home.
- Who do you think Mrs. Lamb is?
- Why was the speaker surprised she gets to take a book home?
- What kind of book is it?

Jose read the whole eighty pages in two hours.
- How long did Jose read?
- How many pages did he read?
- Did Jose finish the book?

Dean ate half of the apple pie with melted cheese on top.
- How much of the pie did Dean eat?
- What kind of pie was it?
- What did it have on top?

Steve wore a cowboy hat; Mike wore a ball cap; Jerry didn't wear a hat.
- What kind of hat did Jerry wear?
- Who wore the cowboy hat?
- What kind of hat did Mike wear?

Marsha moved to Texas last June. Morgan and Evan moved to Iowa at Christmas.
- Who moved to Iowa?
- Who moved in June?
- How many children moved?

0-7682-3121-3 *Creative Reading*

A Memorable Trip to the Zoo

Directions:
1. Read the story below.
2. You may read it as many times as you wish.
3. Next, turn over your paper and draw a picture of the story.
4. Do not look back at the story until your picture is done.
5. Then answer the questions below.

Last night I dreamed I was at the zoo. All the animals were the wrong colors. The leopard was pink with black spots. The zebra had green and orange stripes. There were five snakes. Each snake was pink with red spots. The elephant was blue. And the zoo keeper was wearing a space suit.

1. Did you remember the color of the zebra?

_____

2. Which animals did you color correctly?

_____

3. Did you remember how many snakes there were?

_____

4. Did you draw a zoo keeper in a space suit?

_____

5. Which details did you completely forget?

_____

Sticking Your Neck Out

Directions:

1. Read aloud each paragraph about turtles.
2. Follow each reading with questions that can be answered true or false.
3. Students indicate true by sticking their necks out and false by tucking their heads in like a turtle pulling his head into his shell.

Are Tortoises and Turtles the Same Thing?

The word turtle is used to mean all kinds of turtles: water turtles, sea turtles, box turtles, and tortoises. Tortoises are a special kind of land turtle. All tortoises are turtles, but not all turtles are tortoises.

- All sea turtles are turtles. (T)
- All box turtles are turtles. (T)
- All turtles are tortoises. (F)

What Does a Tortoise Look Like?

A tortoise is a turtle that lives on land. It has a high, domed shell. Tortoises have elephant-shaped hind legs. Tortoises go to water only to drink or bathe.

- Tortoises have birdlike legs. (F)
- Tortoises live in the water. (F)
- Tortoises have high, domed shells. (T)

What's a Group Called?

People who keep pet turtles often say they have a "herd." However, the true term for a group of turtles is a "bale of turtles."

- A group of turtles is sometimes called a "herd." (T)
- The true term for a group of turtles is a "herd of turtles." (F)
- The true term for a group of turtles is a "bale of turtles." (T)

Can Turtles Bite?

It is believed that some prehistoric turtles may have had teeth, but no modern turtles have real teeth. Instead, all of the turtles alive today have very sharp beaks with which they bite.

- Prehistoric turtles may have had teeth. (T)
- Modern turtles have real teeth. (F)
- Turtles bite with very sharp beaks. (T)

Published by Frank Schaffer Publications. Copyright protected. 0-7682-3121-3 *Creative Reading*

Get the Cat Facts

Directions:

1. Read each set of cat facts aloud twice.
2. Then ask questions and give multiple choice answers.
3. Students are to meow like a cat to indicate all correct answers (sometimes there will be more than one correct choice).

Trivia:

- Cats have three eyelids.
- The nose pad of every cat has a ridge pattern as unique as human fingerprints.
- A cat's heart beats twice as fast as a human heart.
- Cats have thirty teeth.

Questions:

1. How many eyelids does a cat have?

    1   2   3

2. All cats have unique patterns on their

    paws   nose   ears

3. How does a cat's heart rate compare to yours?

    same   slower   faster

4. How many teeth do cats have?

    two fangs   ten teeth   thirty teeth

Trivia:

- Almost ten percent of a cat's bones are in its tail.
- An average cat has one to eight kittens per litter.
- In one female cat's lifetime, she can have more than one hundred kittens.
- Cats can make about one hundred sounds—dogs can only make about ten.

Questions:

1. Nearly ten percent of a cat's bones are in its

    legs   body   tail

2. How many kittens are in an average cat's litter?

    1 to 2   1 to 3   1 to 8   1 to 100

3. How many kittens can one cat have in her lifetime?

    more than 20   more than 50   more than 100

4. Dogs have only about ten vocalization sounds. Cats have

    more than 25   more than 50   as many as 100

Read Between the Lines

Materials: "The Three Bears" story (page 69)

Directions:

1. Read the story to the class.

2. Say, "Today we are going to be detectives. We are going to learn how to use clues in a story, along with what we already know, to figure out unwritten answers."

3. Ask questions about the story. Answers should not be in the story but should be such that the students have to make logical conclusions.

   - Which character in the story do you think was the most curious?
   - Did the Bears leave their doors unlocked? How do you know?
   - What was the temperature like? How do you know?
   - Was it a cloudy day? How do you know?
   - Give an example of an act that made Papa Bear seem gruff.
   - Do you think Goldilocks had good or poor manners?
   - Name things Goldilocks did to show bad manners.
   - Why were all three bowls of porridge a different temperature?
   - Which character tried to make peace? Give an example.
   - Do you think the author wanted to represent Goldilocks as a kind character?
   - What kinds of things did Goldilocks do that were unkind?

4. Pair students. Give each a copy of the story.

5. Pairs are to look for clues in the text and make a list of things they can conclude about Goldilocks and each bear.

   Examples:

   Goldilocks—curly hair, blonde, curious, rude, hard to please, hungry, tired, sleepy

   Papa Bear—firm, concerned with family health, careless about locking door, gruff

Published by Frank Schaffer Publications. Copyright protected.
0-7682-3121-3 *Creative Reading*

The Three Bears

One morning at the breakfast table, Papa Bear told Mama Bear and Baby Bear, "Let's go for an early morning stroll."

"Why, I've just poured cream on my porridge," said Mama Bear. "Can't we walk after we eat?"

"No, no, no!" said Papa Bear. "What this family needs is more exercise. We are going to start walking every day."

"But I don't like to walk, Papa," whined Baby Bear as he poured a little cream on his porridge. "My legs are short, and I have to run to keep up with you."

"Don't talk back to your Papa," said Mama Bear, leaving the table. She quickly put on her sweater and said, "Get your coat, Baby Bear. We better take along our umbrellas, too."

Papa Bear opened the big door and the three were on their way.

Shortly after the bears had left, a little girl named Goldilocks came skipping down the path. She went to the door and knocked. When no one answered, she opened the door and yelled inside, "Anyone home?"

She saw beautiful bowls on a long table, chairs, and beds—all in three different sizes—huge, tiny, and middle-sized. *Yum! Something smells good*, she thought.

Goldilocks wondered if the smell was coming from the bowls. She tasted the food in the biggest bowl. *Ouch! Too hot.*

She tasted the food in the middle-sized bowl and it was too cold. But when she tasted the food in the littlest bowl, she found that it was just right. So she sat down in the tiny chair and emptied the bowl. When she had barely finished the porridge, she heard a crack and the chair collapsed beneath her.

Belly full and a bit shaken from the crash to the floor, Goldilocks decided to take a nap. *But which bed?* she thought. The huge bed was wood and looked hard. The middle-sized bed looked way too soft for her taste. But the little bed looked just right. She flopped down and fell fast asleep.

When the bears returned and saw the broken chair and girl sleeping in Baby Bear's bed, they were puzzled. "Who are you?" growled Papa.

Goldilocks was speechless.

Mama Bear said, "Now, dear, calm down. Let the little girl explain."

"She broke my chair," said Baby Bear and he began to cry.

"Out!" growled Papa Bear.

"She ate all my porridge, too," cried Baby Bear.

"I said, get out!" roared Papa.

Goldilocks jumped up and out the door she went, as fast as her little legs would carry her.

0-7682-3121-3 *Creative Reading*

Unhatched Eggs

Materials: Aesop's fable "Unhatched Eggs" (page 71)

Directions:

1. Read the fable to the class.

2. Say, "Today we are going to do more detective work."

3. Ask questions that can be answered only by inferencing.
   - Why did the girl return home empty-handed?
   - Was the girl a creative person? How do you know?
   - Was the girl a careful helper? How do you know?
   - Do you think the girl had a lot of friends?
   - Do you think she had a boyfriend? How do you know?
   - Do you think the girl was rich or poor? What makes you think so?
   - Do you think the girl was afraid of her mother? Why or why not?
   - Do you think the girl's mother was wise?
   - What did the girl do that let you know that her mother would be understanding?
   - What does the saying, "Don't count your chickens before they are hatched" mean?

4. Break into small cooperative groups. Give each a copy of the fable.

5. Students are to make up short skits about what happened next.

6. Allow time for groups to practice the skits.

7. Have students take turns performing skits for the group.

8. On other occasions, practice inferencing skills by having students create dialogue for additional skits based on the fable.
   - girl telling her friends what happened
   - what could have happened in town if she hadn't spilled the milk
   - what could have happened if she had traded the milk for eggs
   - what could have happened if she had found gold on the way home
   - what could have happened if her mother wasn't understanding
   - what could have happened . . .

0-7682-3121-3 *Creative Reading*

Unhatched Eggs

One fine day, an old woman sent her daughter to town to trade their extra milk. "Get something good, like flour, and I will bake us some bread," she told her daughter. "Or potatoes and onions, and I will make us a fine soup. Or a chicken, and I will stew it for our supper."

So off the girl went, carrying the milk in a pail on her head. As she went along, she began dreaming of what she would trade for the milk.

I'll buy live chickens from Farmer White, she thought. The thought pleased her, and she raised her chin a little. And they will lay eggs each morning, she told herself. This pleased the girl even more, and she raised her chin a little higher.

Every day I can take a basket full of eggs to market. She was getting so many ideas. *With the egg money, I'll buy myself a beautiful new dress and a lovely hat.* The girl could almost feel soft velvet on her arms. *I'll buy myself a fabulous hat, too—one with a peacock feather sticking straight up.*

She felt so proud she squared her shoulders and arched her back. *And when I go to market, all the young men will notice my beauty. All the girls will be so jealous, but I won't care. I'll just toss my head like this.*

Alas, when the girl returned that day, tears streaked her cheeks. She didn't have live chickens. She didn't even have flour for baking bread, potatoes or onions for soup, or a chicken for the stew pot. When she told her mother what had gone wrong, the old woman frowned.

Then, slowly, the old woman's frown turned into a smile. "Ah, my sweet daughter. Don't you know it is foolish to count your chickens before they are hatched?"

0-7682-3121-3 *Creative Reading*

The Quack Frog

Preparation: Read the first part of the fable to the class.

The Quack Frog—Aesop Fable

Once there lived a frog that loved to boast and brag. He'd puff himself up big and proclaim to all the beasts that he was a doctor. He claimed to be skilled in the use of herbs found around the marsh and able to heal all diseases. "Not only can I heal, I know the secret of youth. I can tell you what to take to never get old," bragged the frog.

A clever fox, tired of hearing the frog's boasting, put a question to the frog that changed the frog's bragging forever.

Don't read the question to the students. ("How can you pretend to prescribe for others, when you are unable to heal your own wrinkled skin?")

Directions:

1. Break into small cooperative groups.
2. Groups are to discuss and decide what the question was and what will happen next.
3. Each group is to create dialogue and makes up a skit for the fable including their special endings.
4. Allow plenty of time for groups to practice their skits.
5. Then, each small cooperative group performs its skit for the others.
6. List the various outcomes on the board.
7. Compare each group's ending.
8. Ask questions:
    - What question did the fox ask?
    - Which group thought something positive would come out of the frog's bragging?
    - Which skit did you like best? Why?

0-7682-3121-3 *Creative Reading*

Aesop's Fable

Directions: Read the story. Then draw a picture of what you think will happen next.

The Boy and the Nuts

Oliver was a boy who was never full. He ate all day.

One day Oliver found a jar of nuts on the table. He put his hand in the jar. He grabbed a fat fist full of nuts. But when he tried to pull out his hand, it was stuck! It would not fit through the top of the jar. He burst into tears. "My hand is stuck, and I am as hungry as I can be."

His grandfather came into the room. He saw the problem his grandson had. He said, "Be happy with half the nuts in your hand. You will be able to pull out your hand."

In a Nutshell

Preparation: Explain that summarizing is like putting things in a nutshell—saying the facts in as few words as possible. Say, "This kind of writing saves space and is sometimes used by newspaper reporters."

Directions: One at a time, read the long sentences. Ask, "What is the most important message in the sentence?" On the board and with input from students, rewrite each sentence using only the most important words. Try to use ten words or less. (See suggested answers in key.)

1. Aunt Joann, my favorite aunt who lives in Chicago, is coming to stay at our house; since I have an extra bed in my room, she will be sleeping in my room.

2. Robert and his little brother Mickey, who is in kindergarten, rode their bikes to the park to meet me; we played games until nearly dark.

3. When I got home from school, I tried and tried to do my math, but I was hungry and went to the refrigerator for milk and decided I also needed cake; the food made me sleepy so I took a nap.

4. The bus was ten minutes late, and since it was so cold, I decided to go back home and get warm; when I went back to the bus stop the kids were gone, the bus had come and gone, and I had missed it.

They're All Make Believe

Directions:

1. Explain that newspapers often use summarizing statements as titles of stories. They pick the most important and interesting titles to get readers' attention.

2. List the newspaper headlines on the board. One at a time, read aloud.

3. Students are to guess the nursery rhyme or fairy tale associated with each.

Newspaper Headlines:

- Curly-Haired Blonde Breaks and Enters ("Goldilocks and the Three Bears")
- Two Homes Destroyed, a Third Threatened by Heavy Winds ("Three Little Pigs")
- Maiden Awakens from Twenty-Year Coma ("Sleeping Beauty")
- Lost Shoe Results in Marriage of Prince ("Cinderella")
- Boy Breaks Head and Sister Rescues Him ("Jack and Jill")
- Seven Short Men Give Homeless Girl a Home ("Snow White and the Seven Dwarfs")

0-7682-3121-3 *Creative Reading*

Cartoons

Directions: Cartoons are stories told in a sequence of pictures. Summarize a fairy tale, nursery rhyme, or your own story in the six panels. Then show it to friends and see if they can identify the story.

1.	2.
3.	4.
5.	6.

Name _____ **Date** _____

The Slumber Party

Directions: Read the story. Then draw a picture in each circle showing the sequence of events.

The Slumber Party

Marie had a birthday slumber party that began at 6:00. She started getting ready for the party at noon by baking the cake. After the cake was decorated, she and her mother blew up dozens of balloons and decorated the house. At 3:00 Marie set the table. Just before the girls arrived, Marie put on her new party dress. The guests played games and Marie opened her presents before they ate pizza at 9:00. The girls had so much fun, it was almost 11:00 before they all fell asleep.

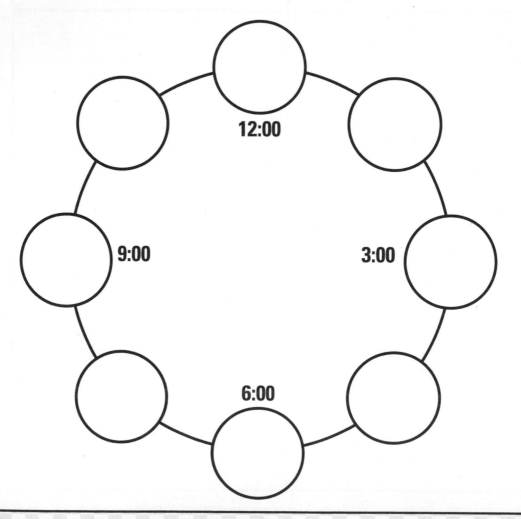

0-7682-3121-3 *Creative Reading*

Make a Cake

Directions: Below are the seven steps for making a cake. Put them in order by putting a number 1–7 in the boxes. Then draw a picture to show each step.

☐ When cake is done, have someone help you remove it from the oven.

☐ Bake as directed on cake mix package.

☐ Wash hands and place all ingredients on a table.

☐ Pour batter into prepared cake pans.

☐ Follow the directions on the package for preparing batter.

☐ Open cake mix box and pour it into a bowl.

☐ Let cake cool and then spread on icing.

Same and Different

Materials: Venn diagram

Preparation: Reproduce page 79 (one per pair of students)

Directions:

1. Ask a boy and girl to come to the front of the class.
2. Draw a Venn diagram on the board.
3. Put the name of each student over a circle.
4. Ask students to name ways the two are different. Each time, list the descriptions in the appropriate circle.
   - boy/girl
   - tall/short
   - wearing jeans/wearing dress (clothes)
   - blonde/red (hair)
5. Next ask for ways they are alike and list these in the overlapping section.
   - blue eyes
   - first graders
   - like to read
6. Explain that you used a diagram to show same and different.
7. Pair students and give them a Venn diagram.
8. Students are to compare and contrast themselves using the diagram.
9. In a large group, have each pair share their diagrams.

Using Venn Diagrams

Directions: Reproduce Venn diagram and have students compare and contrast one or more of the following:

- Compare and contrast Goldilocks and bears.
- Compare and contrast whale and elephant.
- Compare and contrast winter and summer.
- Compare and contrast marshmallow and pillow.
- Compare and contrast people and plants.
- Compare and contrast birds and butterflies.
- Compare and contrast books and TV.
- Compare and contrast mother and father.
- Compare and contrast desert and forest.

0-7682-3121-3 *Creative Reading*

Same and Different

Directions: Write the name of the two things you are comparing on the lines. Then list differences in the outer rings and things that are the same in the overlapping section.

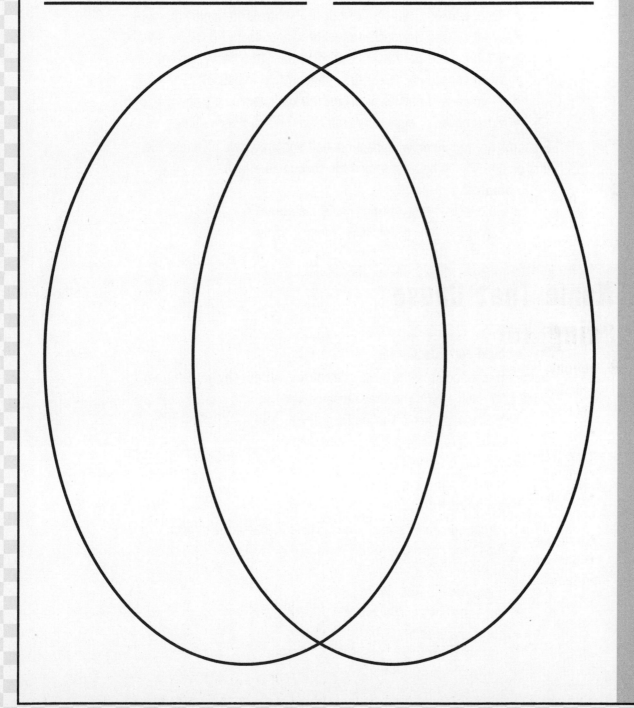

_____ _____

What Caused It?

Materials: "Three Bears" story, drawing paper, crayons or markers

Preparation: Reproduce page 69 (one per student).

Directions:

1. Pass out the story and read it aloud.

2. Ask cause-and-effect questions.
   - What caused the bears to not be home when Goldilocks came to their house? (out walking/needed exercise)
   - What caused Goldilocks to knock on the bears' door? (curiosity)
   - What caused Goldilocks to look in the bowls? (aroma)
   - What caused Goldilocks to feel tired and sleepy? (food/long walk)
   - What caused Baby Bear's chair to break? (too heavy person)
   - What caused Papa Bear to get angry? (girl in house)
   - What caused Baby Bear to cry? (broken chair/empty bowl)
   - What caused Goldilocks to run away? (Papa Bear yelling)

3. Students are to fold drawing paper in half and draw two pictures. The first picture should be a cause and the second an effect.
   Examples:
   - Goldilocks sitting in small chair/chair breaking
   - Papa Bear yelling/Goldilocks running away

Name That Cause

Directions:

1. Play a cause-and-effect game.

2. Name effects and students guess the causes. Accept several different causes for each effect. Encourage creativity.
   - broken egg on the kitchen floor
   - paper torn in tiny pieces in trash can
   - flat tire on school bus
   - flooded bathroom
   - angry truck driver

3. Reverse order and name some causes. Students name the effects.
   - man runs out of gas
   - heavy snow
   - computer breaks down
   - dog eats boy's homework
   - cupboard is empty

0-7682-3121-3 *Creative Reading*

Cause and Effect

Directions: Read each cause and match it with a picture of an effect by writing the correct letter on each blank.

_____ 1. too much water in batter   a.

_____ 2. flying ball   b.

_____ 3. sink overflowed   c.

_____ 4. didn't wipe feet   d.

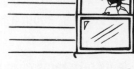

_____ 5. missed nail when hammering   e.

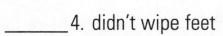

_____ 6. spilled paint   f.

_____ 7. rained all night   g.

_____ 8. ran over nail on bike   h.

0-7682-3121-3 _Creative Reading_

It's a Pig Fact!

Directions:

1. Explain that a fact is something that is true. An opinion is something someone believes—it may be true for that person but not true for everyone.

2. Give an example of a fact. (Count the number of girls in your class.)

3. Give an opinion. (Blue is the prettiest color.)

4. Ask for an example of a fact. Ask for an example of an opinion.

5. Play a fact-or-opinion game. Read the pig trivia and have students say if each is a fact or opinion. Indicate facts with thumbs up and opinions by shrugging shoulders.

Pig Trivia

- I think pigs are one of the most intelligent animals.
- Pigs are distantly related to the hippopotamus family.
- Wild or domestic pigs can be found on every continent except Antarctica.
- Pigs make good pets.
- China has the world's largest population of domestic pigs.
- The average sow gives birth to 8 to 12 pigs at a time.
- Pigs hate it when it rains.
- Pigs don't need to be rounded up. A good yell like "Sooey" will usually bring them running.
- The sound a pig makes is called a "squeal."
- A pig's squeal is an unpleasant sound.
- Pigs look best when they are pink and lean.
- An average pig eats five pounds of feed each day.
- Pigs eat so much, they often make "hogs" of themselves.
- Pigs eat about a ton of food every year.

6. Pair students.

7. Students take turns giving each other facts and opinions about animals.

From Fact to Opinion

Directions:

1. Review the difference between facts and opinions.

2. Name facts.

3. Students are to turn the subject of the fact into an opinion.

    Examples:

    - Sunday always follows Saturday./Sunday is the best day of the week.
    - Popcorn is a sugarless snack./Popcorn is best with butter.
    - Most birds can fly./Birds are fun to watch.
    - Ice cubes make soda colder./Sodas taste best with ice cubes.

0-7682-3121-3 *Creative Reading*

You Decide

Directions: Write "F" for fact and "O" for opinion.

1. Dogs can be pets. _____

2. Small dogs make the best pets. _____

3. Lakes are large bodies of water. _____

4. The lake is pretty at sunset. _____

Directions: Use the subjects in each fact to write an **opinion**.

5. Popcorn is made from corn.

_____

6. Some children like red better than blue.

_____

Directions: Use the subjects in each opinion to write a **fact**.

7. Gray is such a boring color.

_____

8. Bananas are yummy.

_____

0-7682-3121-3 *Creative Reading*

Information Please

Directions:

1. Explain that authors write with a purpose.

2. Name some author purposes: entertain, inform, warn, amuse.

3. One at a time, read a spider trivia. Ask students to decide if the author's purpose is to inform or warn. (Answers may vary.)

Spider Trivia

- The Brown Recluse is known for its poisonous venom. (warn)
- The Brown Recluse will usually bite people only when they are disturbed. (inform/warn)
- The Brown Recluse spins small, loose webs to catch its prey. (inform)
- The female Black Widow is black with the red hourglass on the underside of her abdomen. (inform/warn)
- Of all spiders, the Black Widow is the most frightening. (warn)
- The female's venom is highly poisonous to people. (warn)
- A Black Widow will usually try to run away instead of biting, unless she is guarding her eggs. (inform)
- Wolf spiders are a gray to sand color, with spots of black. (inform)
- Crab spiders walk funny. They hold their legs out to the sides like a crab on the beach and can move forward, sideways, or backwards. (inform)

What's the Purpose?

Directions: Explain that authors often write stories to teach lessons. Read stories that demonstrate examples of stories with lessons.

Examples:

1. Read aloud the story "Goldilocks and the Three Bears" (page 69). Ask students to name a lesson learned.

2. What lesson does the story "The Three Little Pigs" teach?

3. Name a lesson learned in the story "The Little Red Hen."

4. Read aloud Aesop's fable "United We Stand—Divided We Fall" (page 87). Ask students to name a lesson learned.

5. Read aloud Aesop's fable "Goose That Laid Golden Eggs" (page 88). Ask students what message they think the author was trying to convey.

6. Read aloud the play "The Ant and Grasshopper" based upon an Aesop's fable (page 89). Ask students what they think the author's purpose was in telling this tale.

0-7682-3121-3 *Creative Reading*

Reading Signals

Directions: Every road sign has a purpose. Look at each sign. Write its purpose. Use the word bank to help you.

1. _____

2. _____

3. _____

4. _____

5. _____

6. _____

7. _____

8. _____

9. _____

Word Bank:

signal ahead	no U-turn	school zone
watch for sliding rocks	stop	steep hill
bend in road	one way	slippery when wet

You Conclude

Materials: three bags, red and blue cubes (or crayons, paper cut-outs, and so on)

Preparation: place the red cubes in one bag and the blue in the other

Directions:

1. Show students that one bag has red and the other has blue cubes.
2. Pull out a red cube. Ask, "What color will I *always* pull out of this bag?"
3. Pull out a blue cube. Ask, "What color will I *always* pull out of this bag?"
4. Hold up the red bag of cubes. Ask, "What color will I *never* pull out?"
5. Hold up the blue bag of cubes. Ask, "What color will I *never* pull out?"
6. Put one blue cube and one red cube in the third bag. Ask questions.
   - Can I pull out a red cube from this bag?
   - Can I pull out a blue cube from this bag?
   - Pull out the red cube and ask, "Can I pull out another red cube?"
   - Ask, "What color will I pull out?"

Those Are the Facts

Directions:

1. One at a time, read the facts.
2. Ask for conclusions. Answers will vary. Encourage creativity.
   - Amy has three dogs and ten fish. She takes some of her pets for a walk. How many pets does she walk?
   - Albert hates lettuce. The cafeteria is serving bacon, lettuce, and tomato sandwiches on Wednesday. What are the chances that Albert will buy his lunch on Wednesday?
   - Juan always brings two peanut butter and jelly sandwiches in his lunch. Do you think Juan likes peanuts? Why or why not?
   - Morgan and his sister live with their hearing-impaired grandfather. When Morgan is not at home, who answers the telephone?
   - On Friday, Kennedy lost her lunch money on the bus. When she got home from school, she was very hungry. What do you think Kennedy ate for lunch?
   - Marvin's grandmother always gets him what he wants for his birthday. Marvin asked his grandmother for a ticket to the moon. Will he get what he asked for from his grandmother?
   - Half of Cheryl's class is absent—home with the measles. Cheryl notices red blotches on her arms. What is wrong with Cheryl?

0-7682-3121-3 *Creative Reading*

Encore!

Preparation: Read aloud Aesop's fable about the father and his fighting children.

United We Stand—Divided We Fall

A father had three children. They were always fighting. When he could no longer stand the noise, he decided to teach them a lesson.

One day he said, "I want each of you to bring me a thick stick."

They each brought a stick. The father put the three thick sticks together. He tied them with string. Next he told his children to break the sticks in pieces.

One at a time, they tried hard to break the sticks. Not one of them was able to do it.

Then the old man took off the string and pulled the three thick sticks apart. One by one, he placed the sticks into a child's hand. "Now," he said. "Break them."

Soon cracking could be heard and the sticks were easily torn to bits. Still the children did not understand their father's example.

The wise father looked at them and said, "My children, if you work together, you will be as the bundle of sticks—safe from your enemies. But if you fight among yourselves, you will be broken as easily as you have broken the sticks."

Directions:

1. Break into groups of four.
2. Students are to dramatize the story. Allow time for students to practice.
3. Share skits in large group.

Dramatizations

Materials: Aesop's fable "Goose That Laid Golden Eggs"

Preparation: Reproduce page 88 for each student.

Directions:

1. Students are to silently read the fable.
2. Break into small cooperative groups and have students turn the fable into a skit.
3. Allow time to practice skits.
4. Share skits in large group.

Goose That Laid Golden Eggs

Directions: Read the Aesop fable. Get two friends (one to play the narrator). Turn the story into a skit.

Goose That Laid Golden Eggs

One day a man found a yellow egg in his goose's nest. When he picked it up, it was heavy. At first he was going to throw it away. He thought his wife was playing a trick. But when he showed it to her, she said, "This is not a trick. Look, this egg is pure gold!"

The man took a closer look. Yes, it was pure gold.

The next day the man and his wife went to the goose's nest. The same thing was there—a golden egg.

They stayed up all night, waiting for the goose to lay another egg. When it did, it was gold once again.

Day after day, the goose laid a golden egg. Soon the couple was rich. But as they grew richer, they grew more and more greedy.

"Wife," he said, "I cannot wait for that slow goose to lay the eggs. Tonight I am going to cut it open and get all the gold at once."

"What a good idea," said his wife. "I will help." But they did not find any gold.

"What have we done?" cried the wife.

"We've killed the goose that laid golden eggs," said the man.

And the couple lived unhappily ever after.

0-7682-3121-3 *Creative Reading*

The Ant and the Grasshopper

Directions: Read the play based upon an Aesop's fable. Make the stick puppets on page 90 and use them to put on a puppet show.

Ant: What a fine winter day. I will dry the grain I got last summer.

Grasshopper: Hello, Ant.

Ant: What do you want, Grasshopper?

Grasshopper: Only to say hi.

Ant: But you were too busy singing last summer to say hello.

Grasshopper: Oh, Ant, it was you who were too busy for me. You were working. That is why I did not say hi. I only come in friendship now.

Ant: I do not trust you, Grasshopper. What do you want?

Grasshopper: I would not ask this if I were not so hungry. Please, Ant, can you give me a little bit of food? I am starving and there is no grain in the fields.

Ant: You came to beg for food? Why did you not save food during the summer?

Grasshopper: Oh, Ant, I was busy passing the days in singing.

Ant: Well, then, if you were foolish enough to sing all summer, you must dance to bed in the winter without supper.

0-7682-3121-3 *Creative Reading*

Ant and Grasshopper Puppets

Directions:

1. Color the ant and grasshopper.
2. Cut out.
3. Attach each to a craft stick.
4. Get behind a large cardboard box, sofa, or chair draped with material, and hold puppets up so the class can see them but not you.
5. Read the script on page 89.

0-7682-3121-3 *Creative Reading*

Who What? When Where? Why? How?

Materials: index cards, paper, pencils

Preparation: Write *who, what, when, where, why,* or *how* on index cards—enough so that each student will have one.

Directions:

1. Explain that many words tell: who, what, when, where, why, or how. On the board, write examples of each.
   - Who—Old McDonald, Little Boy Blue. Have students with "who" cards hold them up.
   - What—farm, cow. Have students with "what" cards hold them up.
   - When—now, tomorrow. Have students with "when" cards hold them up.
   - Where—here, there. Have students with "where" cards hold them up.
   - Why—liked animals, sleepy. Have students with "why" cards hold them up.
   - How—happily, quickly. Have students with "how" cards hold them up.

2. Give words or phrases and students with the appropriate cards hold them up.

   Examples:
   - The bear (pause for "what") went (pause for "what") over the mountain. (pause for "where")
   - The wheels (pause for "what") on the bus (pause for "where") went round and round.

3. Pair students. Have each pair make a list of whos, whats, whens, wheres, whys, and hows.

When? How? Why?

Directions:

1. Say, "He broke his leg." Then ask, "When?" Students are to volunteer a variety of answers. List on the board under "When?"

when he was seven	yesterday
before our vacation	last summer

2. Say, "He broke his leg." Then ask, "How?" List responses in a new column.

water skiing	in a car accident
falling out of a tree	in a bike crash

3. Say, "He broke his leg." Then ask, "Why?" List responses in a new column.

because he wasn't careful	because he wasn't wearing a seat belt
because he was clumsy	because he was distracted

0-7682-3121-3 *Creative Reading*

Who-a-What? Who-a-What? Where?

Directions:

1. To review who, what, and where, teach students the new version of "Old MacDonald Had a Farm."

2. Divide into two groups. First group sings "Old MacDonald Had a Farm," pausing after phrases. Second group shouts *who, what, when, where,* or *why* at appropriate times. Instead of singing E-I-E-I-O, everyone sings: Who-a-what? Who-a-what? Where?

Old MacDonald Had a Farm

Group #1—Old MacDonald

Group #2—Who?

Group #1—had a farm.

Group #2—A-What?

Everyone sings—Who-a-what? Who-a-what? Where?

Group #1—And on his farm.

Group #2—WHERE?

Group #1—He had a cow.

Group #2—A-WHAT?

Everyone sings: Who-a-what? Who-a-what? Where?

Group #1—With a moo, moo here.

Group #2—A-WHAT? WHERE?

Group #1—And a moo, moo there.

Group #2—A-WHAT? WHERE?

Group #1—Here a moo.

Group #2—WHERE? A-WHAT?

Group #1—There a moo.

Group #2—WHERE? A-WHAT?

Group #1—Everywhere a moo, moo.

Group #2—WHERE? A-WHAT?

Group #1—Old MacDonald

Group #2—WHO?

Group #1—had a farm.

Group #2—A-WHAT?

Everyone sings—Who-a-what? Who-a-what? Where?

3. If students enjoy the song, sing with other animals and animal sounds.

0-7682-3121-3 *Creative Reading*

Dissecting a Rhyme

Directions: Read a nursery rhyme or story. Fill in the title. List as many *whos, whats, wheres, whens, whys,* and *hows* as you can.

Title _____

Who?
What?
Where?
When?
Why?
How?

0-7682-3121-3 *Creative Reading*

Verbal-Linguistic Intelligence
Logical-Mathematical Intelligence
Bodily-Kinesthetic Intelligence
Visual-Spatial Intelligence
Musical Intelligence
Interpersonal Intelligence
Intrapersonal Intelligence
Naturalist Intelligence

Answer Key

Page 55

yellow bat, green duck, purple raccoon, red frog, blue pig, green skunk, orange hen, pink zebra, red dog, blue mule, purple snail, yellow cat

Page 56

1. mule
2. Grandma
3. hay wagon
4. seven
5. barn loft
6. cat
7. two
8. red
9. hay
10. nine

Page 57

1. blue scissors
2. red apple
3. purple kite
4. green tree and frog
5. cake with pink icing and red candles
6. white marshmallow and snowflake
7. orange ring around cake, marshmallow and apple (perhaps a frog, too)

Page 74

1. Aunt Joann will come and sleep in my room.
2. Robert, Mickey, and I played in the park.
3. I ate and slept instead of doing math homework.
4. I missed the bus because I went home.

Page 77

6. When cake is done, have someone help you remove it from the oven.
5. Bake as directed on cake mix package.
1. Wash hands and place all ingredients on a table.
4. Pour batter into prepared cake pans.
3. Follow the directions on the package for preparing batter.
2. Open cake mix box and pour it into a bowl.
7. Let cake cool and then spread on icing.

Page 81

1. h
2. e
3. b
4. g
5. a
6. d
7. f
8. c

Page 85

1. stop
2. bend in road
3. steep hill
4. school zone
5. slippery when wet
6. no U-turn
7. one way
8. watch for sliding rocks
9. signal ahead

0-7682-3121-3 Creative Reading

CERTIFICATE OF AWARD

This is to certify that

_____

is great at
PHONICS!

Date _____

Signature _____

CERTIFICATE OF AWARD

This is to certify that

_____

can read
SIGHT WORDS!

Date _____

Signature _____

0-7682-3121-3 *Creative Reading*

CERTIFICATE OF AWARD

This is to certify that

_____

has great
LISTENING SKILLS!

Date _____

Signature _____

CERTIFICATE OF AWARD

This is to certify that

_____

has great
READING COMPREHENSION!

Date _____

Signature _____

0-7682-3121-3 *Creative Reading*